58278

CANTERBURY COLLEGE
NEW DOVER ROAD, CANTERBURY

LEARNING RESOURCES CENTRE

Tel: 01227 811166

Please return book on or before date last stamped:

10 FEB 2000		
18 JAN 2002		
0 6 APR 2011		
0 9 JAN 2015		
2 8 JAN 2020		
0 3 FEB 2020		
2 1 OCT 2020		

The Community

Canterbury (

ISBN 1-899308-06-7

Cover design by Design Hive

Typeset and designed by
Word Perfect, Christchurch, Dorset.

Printed in Great Britain

CONTENTS

Note to Reader

About the Author

Dr. Leonard Mervyn is a Clinical Biochemist, experienced in pharmaceutical research and with a special interest in Vitamins and Minerals. He was the first to discover Coenzyme Q10 in man and identified the active form of vitamin B12, methylcobalamin, in human blood. He has written many books and scientific papers and has been honoured both by a Cressy Morrison Award from the New York Academy of Sciences and by an Italseber Gold Medal from the University of Pavia. He is currently the Technical Director of a major Healthcare Company, and is both a fellow of The Royal Society of Chemistry and The Royal Society of Health. In addition to his other interests, Dr. Mervyn is an external examiner for Oxford University.

1 | Introduction

In Europe it has been shown by market research that between 10 and 15% of the population take some sort of vitamin/mineral supplement on a regular basis. Yet in North America at least 40% of the US population already take vitamin/mineral supplements of which 53% are 'multi' and 41% are specific micro nutrient preparations. These are taken in the main as preventive measures against the serious diseases of later life but many are taken also to replenish vitamins and minerals lost to excess by various lifestyles. Although the perfect diet would provide 215mg vitamin C, 23mg vitamin E, 6mg beta-carotene, 350µg folic acid and 1000 mg calcium with recommended Dietary Allowances (RDA's) of all the other vitamins and minerals, such figures are achievable only through supplementation either by tablets or fortification of foods.

The limiting nutrients in the typical American and European diets are folic acid, vitamin B6, magnesium and zinc. Second limiting are calcium, iron and the carotenoid sources of vitamin A. Economists have estimated that improved intakes of certain micro nutrients, in particular the antioxidants vitamin C, vitamin E and beta-carotene, would decrease healthcare costs by 25% for cardiovascular disease; by 16-30% for a variety of major cancers and by 50% for eye cataract conditions. These translate into billions of dollars of healthcare cost savings per annum. Adequate intakes of the necessary micro nutrients could be achieved by full restoration of the nutrient losses attributable to the refinement of wheat, corn and rice flour by adding the appropriate vitamins and minerals to the refined foods. In addition, the needs for antioxidant nutrients which are far and above the dietary provision can only be achieved by tablet or capsule supplementation.

Supplemental use of vitamins to prevent disease is becoming more and more apparent . The efficacy of such use, or even the trend for intakes above that which can be supplied by means of diet alone, has been the source of considerable controversy in the medical and scientific fields. Recently published data has given strong support to several of the claims for major benefits of disease prevention, including that of cancer, cardiovascular disease, carpal tunnel syndrome and neural tube defects, to name just a few. The purported benefits for supplemental vitamin usage are discussed as well as how vitamins can complement medical therapy of these diseases.

Recent discoveries from the field of research include:

(i) How you may diagnose mild deficiencies of vitamins when induced by bad diets or one's own lifestyle.

(ii) How the RDAs are designed for levels of vitamin intake which can be achieved by means of diet, not for those wishing to prevent chronic diseases by means of vitamin supplementation.

(iii) Supplemental intakes of the antioxidant vitamins (C,E and beta-carotene) have been shown to reduce the risk of specific types of cancers and cardiovascular diseases.

(iv) Supplemental vitamin B6 may prevent the onset of carpal tunnel syndrome.

(v) Supplemental nicotinic acid, but not niacinamide, is effective in lowering blood cholesterol levels, especially that of low-density lipoprotein cholesterol.

(vi) Supplemental folic acid to women of childbearing age can reduce the risk of neural tube defects but poses the real risk of masking pernicious anaemia in the elderly.

One of the most bewildering aspects of vitamin and mineral supplementation to the average person is the vast range of potencies of these nutrients on display in any health food store and in some pharmacies. These products can be classed within three different levels of potency, each of which has a logical reason for taking it and so simplifying the process of selection.

The first of these can be described as products containing a comparatively low potency of ingredients and hence known as the Insurance level. These are usually present in at least 100% of the Recommended Daily Allowance but may rise to 200 or 300%. They are simply meant to top up any mild deficiency of nutrients due to inadequate diets of one sort or another. The intake is usually one capsule or tablet daily and this will ensure an adequate amount of ingredients for any individual without reference to those micro nutrients taken in the diet. These products are no substitute for a good diet but at least will guarantee there is no vitamin or mineral deficiency.

The second level of supplementation is what I call the 'Lifestyle' level and the potencies of the ingredients are usually between 400 and 500% of the RDA but may reach 1000% in some cases. The level is taken by those whose lifestyles require more vitamins than can be met even by a good diet. Such individuals may lead very stressful lives, can be tobacco smokers and/or drinkers of alcohol, are undergoing medical therapy on prescribed drugs (or simply taking the contraceptive pill) or are athletically minded with high physical activity. These are all lifestyle factors which can demand increased turnover of vitamins that cannot be met from the food.

The third level of supplementation is what I call the Therapeutic level. These are vitamins that are taken at high, though absolutely safe, intakes because they are acting as therapeutic drugs rather than vitamins. This aspect of supplementation is becoming more popular as research groups continue to report how vitamins can often complement conventional medicinal drug therapy in treating certain diseases.

I must add also that in the UK at least, every vitamin supplement on sale to the general public can be considered safe, even on long term usage, as long as it is taken in accordance with the instructions on the pack.

Note

1 gram (g) = 1000 milligrams (mg)
1 milligram (mg) = 1000 micrograms (µg)
1 kilogram (kg) = 1000 grams (g)

2 | Signs and Symptoms of Vitamin Deficiency

What happens when we don't receive sufficient of any of these vitamins? To answer this question we need to look at the difference between what is termed a gross deficiency, where the consequences may be life-threatening, and milder deficiencies where the consequences may be a feeling of 'under-the-weather' or, to steal another phrase, 'one degree under'. It is important to realise that the symptoms associated with a gross lack of vitamins may present themselves in a milder form with a less serious deficiency. Hence treatment is similar, namely replacement of the vitamin in short supply. We shall consider later how mild deficiencies may manifest themselves, but let us look at the gross deficiency disease.

We are very fortunate in the West that the diseases associated with serious deficiencies of various vitamins rarely present themselves, but they do exist in the world as a whole. Many thousands of people, particularly children, still go blind in Africa, Asia and South America because of vitamin A deficiency. Rickets, a disease specifically associated with lack of vitamin D, has reappeared in Britain amongst the Asian immigrant population. New-born babies, particularly premature ones, are increasingly being given small intramuscular injections of vitamins E and K, to control the effects of excess oxygen and to prevent haemorrhage respectively – problems that may manifest themselves in the first few days of life. Vitamin B12 deficiency, usually due to an inability to absorb the vitamin, is still a world-wide problem. The end-result is pernicious anaemia, a killing form of anaemia, that is insidious in its onset.

Scurvy, once the scourge of sailors on long voyages, prevalent until less than 100 years ago, still reappears in early spring in elderly people in the northern hemispheres, and is due entirely to low intakes of vitamin C. Beriberi, induced by lack of thiamine (vitamin B1) is still the cause of death of many in the Third World although, mercifully, it is almost unknown in the West. Pellagra is a fatal disease that killed many thousands of Americans in the Southern states of the USA as recently as the 1920's. It was this tragedy that stimulated the American authorities to seek a reason for its prevalence. The culmination of their research was the demonstration that its prevention and cure was easily manifested by a substance called nicotinic acid – a chemical that had been known for more than 50 years at that time. Despite our knowledge on the relationship between pellagra and nicotinic acid, the disease still kills many thousands worldwide each year. In the UK, folic acid deficiency still represents a potential hazard in pregnancy, and recent research suggests a possible relationship between low maternal levels of the vitamin and the incidence of spina bifida in babies. The Department of Health now recommends increased intakes of folic acid by all women who are pregnant or contemplating pregnancy.

We need not feel complacent about not experiencing vitamin deficiency in the West, despite the fact that diseases due to gross deficiency are relatively rare. What is of more concern are those minor complaints that could be associated with a mild lack of certain vitamins. We shall consider these now but, before we do so, it is important to point out there is a growing belief amongst nutritionists, biochemists and some medical doctors that vitamin intake, and hence need, falls into two categories. In the first, low intake, there is just sufficient to prevent the signs and symptoms of gross vitamin deficiency from appearing. In the second, higher intake, there are sufficient vitamins to maintain optimum health. What most of us are getting is a vitamin intake somewhere in between these two levels. There are dietary means and perhaps supplementary treatment with vitamins to ensure that our intakes are at those required for optimum health. At the same time, we should not lose sight of the individual requirements of individuals in respect of their vitamin needs. Careful selection of supplementary vitamins may be required to satisfy particular demands by some people.

Symptoms possibly associated with vitamin deficiency

Mild abnormalities that may be associated with less serious deficiencies of vitamins are now being recognised in certain sectors of the population. Discrete areas of the body provide useful information to the individual so that with proper interpretation a clue to dietary deficiencies due to poor nutrition is given. At the same time, a superficial knowledge of what various vitamins do can indicate an associated possible deficiency if that particular function is affected. For example, the three B vitamins – thiamine, riboflavin and nicotinamide (or niacin) – are all concerned with the conversion of food to energy. Lack of energy may be due to mild deficiencies of these vitamins. Pyridoxine is the anti-depressant vitamin so any mild depressive state may respond to this vitamin. Pantothenic acid and biotin appear to have anti-stress functions so their intake should be increased in any stressful situation. Both vitamin B12 and folic acid are concerned with production of blood cells so they are useful factors in treating certain types of anaemia, themselves often a cause of tiredness and lack of energy. These are all symptoms that an individual can detect themselves, although professional help is essential to determine whether an anaemia is due to lack of vitamin B12 or of folic acid.

The more obvious areas affected by vitamin deficiencies are the skin, the mouth and the eyes but some symptoms of the gastro-intestinal tract and the nerves are also obvious to the individual affected. Many of these afflictions will respond to self-help in terms of improved diet or vitamin supplementation. Changes in the blood, the blood vessels, the heart, the bones, the brain and the reproductive systems that are associated with vitamin deficiency may require professional diagnosis. However, once diagnosis has been made, the individual can still confidently complement other treatments with improved diet and supplementary therapy as in heart disease, for example, where vitamin E, lecithin and fish oils will act in conjunction with conventional medical treatment.

The Skin

Animal studies have provided much of our knowledge-on how vitamin deficiencies can affect the skin and in some cases these translate also to the human being.

VITAMIN A

The skin does appear to be sensitive to vitamin A deficiency which can manifest itself as a hard, stippled skin known as toad skin. There may also be small, raised lesions that are hard and deeply pigmented in deficiency of this vitamin. There are many minor skin complaints like acne, eczema and psoriasis that respond in some cases to vitamin A treatment. This may be given orally or applied directly as an ointment to the afflicted area or both. The excellent response that has been obtained suggests that vitamin A deficiency, even a localised one, may be a factor in the development of these skin irritations.

VITAMIN C

Tiny haemorrhages beneath the skin, known as petechiae, that appear to be scattered over a wide area are characteristic of vitamin C deficiency. In addition, hardened pimples sometimes appear over the hair follicles of the calves and buttocks if body vitamin levels are low. The hairs too are affected, taking on a spiral shape or failing to appear.

VITAMIN E

The development of unsightly scars and striae (stretch marks) may be a feature of mild vitamin E deficiency since such skin problems have been overcome or prevented by taking vitamin E orally and by applying the vitamin in a cream or ointment base directly to the affected skin.

VITAMIN K

Purple patches under the skin, known as purpura, may reflect a blood-clotting problem. Vitamin K is necessary for the normal clotting of blood and a deficiency may present with purple patches. Self-treatment of this condition is usually dietary since the vitamin is not usually available on general sale.

VITAMIN B COMPLEX

Adequate intakes of all these vitamins are needed for a healthy skin, so not surprisingly, this tissue is amongst the first to be affected by even a mild deficiency. When pyridoxine (vitamin B6) *is* lacking the result is a dry, scaly skin with an excessive looseness resulting in a loss of body hair. The condition of seborrhoea, induced by an excessive secretion of the sebaceous glands of the skin, is seen about the eyes, nose, lips and mouth, sometimes extending to the eyebrows and ears, when pyridoxine intakes are low. Other obvious signs are redness of the moist surfaces of the body; a scaly and pigmented dermatitis is often seen around the neck, forearms, elbows and thighs.

Deficiency of riboflavin (vitamin B2) produces typical skin lesions manifested, in the main, by cracking of the lips and cracks in the corners of the mouth, the condition known as Cheilosis. Dermatitis, characterised by a red, itchy skin with the development of small blisters, is often a feature of riboflavin deficiency particularly in the areas of the nose, lips and genitals. Ulcers may appear on the lips and wet surfaces of the body.

Gross deficiency of nicotinic acid or nicotinamide (vitamin B3) leads to the serious disease pellagra, one of the characteristics of which is a rough, horny skin. This starts with a temporary redness, rather like sunburn, which clears to produce a more severe coloration in the form of deep red spots. These coalesce to form a dark, red or purple eruption followed by scaling and loss of skin, the areas most affected are the face, neck, hands and feet – on the hands the condition is called 'pellagrous glove'. Milder deficiency of the vitamin can also produce similar skin problems, not perhaps to the same extent, but characteristic nevertheless.

Pantothenic acid (vitamin B5) deficiency can produce 'burning feet' sensations on the soles where the skin feels to be hot and sore and it is difficult to put the foot down. Some of the skin symptoms associated with riboflavin deficiency may also clear up with pantothenic acid therapy, suggesting that they are a result of a lack of both vitamins. When pantothenic acid is lacking in some animals, skin ulceration and greying of hair result. Human beings do not usually show such signs but occasionally both have responded to supplementary pantothenic acid.

In infants, deficiency of the B vitamin biotin produces a localised, scaly, shedding dermatitis that responds only to this vitamin. Adults are less likely to suffer a similar skin condition due to biotin deficiency because the bacteria that inhabit the lower end of the intestine produce ample quantities of the vitamin. Infants may have a population of intestinal bacteria which has not developed enough to avail themselves of this facility.

The Mouth

Although we shall deal with how lack of individual vitamins affects the mouth, the symptoms may be more indicative of a generalised deficiency and treatment of oral lesion is usually best dealt with by the whole of the vitamin B complex and vitamin C. When riboflavin is lacking the first signs are a sore tongue with cracking of the lips and of the angles of the mouth, usually accompanied by intractable mouth ulcers. The tongue takes on a characteristic magenta colour with deep fissures and raised areas known as papillae.

In nicotinic acid deficiency the tongue will be swollen and the colour of raw beef. Other parts of the mouth affected include the gums, the mouth and the tongue, all of which become inflamed. An inflamed tongue may also be indicative of pyridoxine deficiency but in other respects, lack of the vitamin causes cracking of the lips and of the corners of the mouth — conditions also associated with low intakes of riboflavin.

The smooth, sore tongue associated with vitamin B12 deficiency is almost diagnostic of the condition. An inability to absorb the vitamin may give rise to pernicious anaemia. This serious complaint will only respond to vitamin B12 and treatment is only by intramuscular injection of the vitamin. A generalised low dietary intake of vitamin B12 now common in vegetarians and particularly vegans, will usually affect the tongue early on in the deficiency and healing is rapid once the vitamin is supplied in the diet.

Although we tend to associate disorders of the mouth and tongue with a possible vitamin B complex deficiency, lack of vitamin C is also a likely cause of such lesions. In low vitamin C intakes there are bleeding gums, which can become inflamed, leading to a loosening of the teeth. Small localised haemorrhages may also appear in the mouth. As we saw above, biotin deficiency is more likely in the infant because of its immature intestinal bacterial population. When the specific skin dermatitis appears, this may continue into the mouth, causing rawness on its surface. The condition will respond only to biotin.

The Gastro-Intestinal Tract

The digestive system can be affected by vitamin B complex deficiency at

any level. Diarrhoea can be due to many causes but it is also a feature of thiamine or nicotinic acid deficiency. If thiamine is lacking, the diarrhoea is usually accompanied by abdominal distension and stomach pains. In the absence of any other obvious cause of persistent diarrhoea, the possibility of a vitamin B complex deficiency should always be considered and the appropriate therapy started.

Pantothenic acid deficiency has been shown to cause temporary paralysis of the intestinal tract, particularly when this occurs in the post-operative state. The condition is known as paralytic ileus and it is characterised by abdominal distress and distension, sometimes with the inability to pass motions. It is, therefore, a sensible precaution to ensure the body levels of pantothenic acid are adequate in the period before undergoing an abdominal operation, to reduce the chances of developing paralytic ileus.

The Eyes

When certain vitamins are lacking, both the process of sight and the health of the eye tissues can be adversely affected. Night blindness is a specific symptom of vitamin A deficiency that is characterised by poor adaptation of the eyes to low-intensity light conditions. Vision is normal under bright daylight or artificial light conditions but is lost in the dark. In the absence of the vitamin eye tissues also become abnormal – they are dry and thickened, particularly in the cornea or white of the eye and in the conjunctiva or wet membrane of the eye.

The white of the eye is also affected by riboflavin deficiency – it becomes bloodshot due to minute haemorrhages of the blood vessels. Other features are conjunctivitis or inflammation of the wet membranes particularly in the lower eyelid; a feeling of grittiness in the eye; a constant watering of the eye. Failing vision may occur if the deficiency worsens.

Thiamine (vitamin B1) deficiency is most likely to give rise to a dimness of vision that cannot be associated with a specific condition of the eye. The eye muscles too are affected by low levels of the vitamin. There are often involuntary rhythmic movements of the eyeballs, known as nystagmus, fatigue of the eye muscles and paralysis of the eye resulting in reduced clearness of vision. Similar lesions are seen in nicotinic acid deficiency; which suggests that they may be associated more with a generalised vitamin B complex lack rather than a specific one.

Haemorrhages inside the eye often appear in vitamin C deficiency before they are obvious on the skin. Similarly when vitamin K levels are low, as in new-born babies, the first signs are haemorrhages in the retina of the eye. Similar lesions are observed in adults also, but deficiency of the vitamin is more likely in the new-born. This is because vitamin K does

not readily pass across the placenta from mother to child and the intestinal bacteria of the new-born are not developed sufficiently to supply the vitamin from that source. Hence, as in the case of the B vitamin biotin, the new-born baby is also at risk of vitamin K deficiency.

The Central Nervous System

The normal metabolism of the nerves and brain depends upon adequate intakes of all the members of the vitamin B complex. Hence, deficiency of one or more of these vitamins will give rise to symptoms affecting the nervous system. When thiamine levels are low, mental confusion results leading eventually to coma. Milder deficiency causes involuntary rhythmic movement of the eyeballs (nystagmus) and this is one of the first signs. Other obvious mental symptoms include confabulation (narration of exaggerated fictitional experiences) and a generalised nerve inflammation that results in foot and wrist drop, due to lack of nervous control of the appropriate muscles.

When pyridoxine is low in infants the consequence is often the appearance of convulsions. This is because the vitamin is essential in the production of the brain substance GABA (gamma aminobutyric acid), which normally has a calming effect upon brain function. When it is lacking, control is lost and convulsions result. In adults, lack of pyridoxine more often manifests itself in mild depression and in generalised inflammation of the nerves, leading to tingling, numbness, burning pain and loss of vibratory sensation.

A similar generalised inflammation of the nerves is an early feature of nicotinic acid deficiency, but, in addition, an inflammatory condition of brain, known as encephalopathy, also appears. This becomes worse as the deficiency develops further, leading to a progressive dementia characterised by apprehension, confusion, derangement and maniacal outbursts.

Although the first detectable sign of vitamin B12 deficiency is often anaemia, a progressive nervous degeneration eventually manifests itself. The symptoms are pins and needles in the feet and hands, weakness in the limbs, stiffness in the legs leading to unsteadiness, lethargy and easy fatigue. In advanced deficiency, mental confusion and delirium are often seen, particularly in the aged. Reflexes are depressed leading to slow reactions and there is often an impairment of the sensation of touch. The tragedy is that although the anaemia associated with vitamin B12 deficiency is readily reversed by injection of the vitamin, a stage in nervous degeneration can be reached which is irreversible. Because of this, if any of the symptoms mentioned above appear, it is absolutely essential that professional diagnosis and treatment of the condition of

vitamin B12 deficiency is undertaken at the earliest opportunity. When folic acid is deficient in the body, the only mental symptom likely to be encountered is mental derangement whereby the individual is confused and lacks the ability to describe events, and is unaware of any abnormality. Professional guidance is essential to distinguish between folic acid and vitamin B12 deficiencies since correct diagnosis is essential before the appropriate therapy can be undertaken.

The Blood

Deficiencies of vitamins can also induce changes in other parts of the body. Unlike those discussed above, which may be obvious to the individual, these other changes are usually detected only in clinical examinations. The blood is amongst those tissues affected by the lack of specific vitamins which can result in anaemia of various types. Symptoms of anaemia, of whatever type, are similar and include paleness, tiredness, lethargy, breathlessness, weakness, vertigo, headache, constant noises in the head (tinnitus), spots before the eyes, drowsiness, irritability, cessation of periods, loss of libido and sometimes low-grade fever. Occasionally, there are gastro-intestinal complaints, and even heart failure can develop. Correct treatment of the particular type of anaemia requires correct diagnosis which must be left to the medical practitioner. However, by looking to your intake of the vitamins required to prevent anaemia, you can at least ensure against developing the condition which is induced by their deficiency.

When the red blood cells are depleted of the oxygen-carrying substance known as haemoglobin the resulting condition is called hypochromic anaemia. Sometimes the red blood cells are also smaller than usual, when the condition is known as microcytic hypochromic anaemia. This type of anaemia may be caused by a deficiency of either pyridoxine or riboflavin or even both. Megaloblastic anaemia is of a completely different type where the red blood cells are deprived of haemoglobin and are irregular in size. Lots of immature red blood cells, which are not capable of carrying oxygen, also appear in the blood. The most likely cause of megaloblastic anaemia is a lack of vitamin B12 or folic acid, or of both vitamins.

The most common type of anaemia is that due to iron deficiency. Iron occupies an essential, central role in haemoglobin – in fact oxygen is carried on the back of the iron in haemoglobin. Iron cannot be absorbed from the food or from supplements without vitamin C, so deficiency of this vitamin may also give rise to iron-deficient anaemia. At the same time in the absence of vitamin C, iron cannot be incorporated into the haemoglobin protein. Lack of vitamin C, as we have seen, can also cause loss of blood through haemorrhage so this too can contribute to the development of anaemia. Even when iron is adequate in the diet, unless it is accompanied by sufficient vitamin C, it cannot be efficiently absorbed and utilised. In fact, many researchers believe that if we all had adequate intakes of vitamin C, we would all make better use of the iron in our diets even when intake of the mineral was low.

Lack of vitamin E in the blood can give rise to what is known as haemolytic anaemia. In this condition the red blood cells are weakened to such an extent that they burst easily, spilling their content of haemoglobin into the blood. Once haemoglobin has left the red blood cell it no longer has the capacity to carry oxygen. Hence, if too many red blood cells burst, the oxygen–carrying function of the blood is severely reduced and symptoms of anaemia result. Adequate vitamin E intakes will prevent haemolytic anaemia by toughening up the membranes of the red blood cells which hold them together.

The Heart and Blood Vessels

Thiamine deficiency in the later stages causes severely weakened heart muscle which can lead to heart failure. Gross enlargement of the heart is also a feature of thiamine deficiency. A different effect upon the heart and blood vessels is manifested by pyridoxine deficiency. Massive fat deposits are laid down in the walls of these organs, leading to the condition, known as atherosclerosis, which severely restricts the flow of blood. As the insidious process continues, the ultimate result is complete deprivation of blood, and hence oxygen, to the heart muscle itself when heart failure is inevitable.

The Bones

Pain in the bones can be related to some vitamin deficiencies but as the condition can also be due to other factors, diagnosis of the cause of bone pain is best left to the medical practitioner who can enlist the aid of X-rays and other techniques. Nevertheless, vitamin C in high doses has been used to reduce bone pain. Lack of vitamin D, in both adults and children, can cause bone problems which will respond only to treatment with the vitamin. As the deficiency in most of these cases is simply lack of dietary vitamin D, sometimes combined with deprivation of sunlight on the body, the remedy is obvious – ensure the diet contains vitamin D-rich foods and try to spend some time out in the fresh air. The conditions induced by low vitamin D intakes are rickets in children and osteomalacia in adults.

The Reproductive System

Most of our knowledge on the effect of vitamin deficiencies on the reproductive system of both males and females has come from animal studies. The two most important vitamins in this respect are B12 and E although recent reports suggest that lack of vitamin C can cause less fertile male spermatozoa. In the male of the species, lack of these vitamins causes decreased production and mobility of the sperm leading, in extreme deficiency, to sterility. In the female, conception is still possible when intakes of these vitamins are low, but the offspring rarely reach full term. There are scattered reports that both vitamin E and B12 have helped some couples to conceive when their previous inability to do so was due to mild deficiency of the vitamins. However, there is a lack of hard evidence that vitamin deficiency plays a major role in causing sterility and infertility in people, despite some small success with vitamin therapy and the fact that animals have a need for adequate vitamin intake for full reproductive capacity.

We have seen in this chapter how self-examination or the observation of others can give a clue to possible deficiencies of specific vitamins in the body. The reasons why we may not be getting our full complement of these essential micro nutrients are many and varied. The choice of food; the way it is cooked, processed and stored; the amount eaten are all contributory factors in determining vitamin intake. In addition, lifestyles, social habits, diseases, pregnancy, medicinal drugs and other stresses may increase daily requirements of vitamins, often to levels above those that can be obtained even in an excellent diet. Little wonder then that many individuals existing on barely adequate intakes of vitamins will develop deficiency symptoms when their circumstances change under the influence of the factors mentioned above.

SUMMARY TABLE

Signs and Symptoms of Vitamin Deficiency

Affected Area	*Signs/Symptoms*	*Possible Vitamin Deficiency*
General	Fatigue, malaise, apathy, depression	Usually B complex
	Loss of appetite	Vitamin B1, vitamin B12
Nervous System	Headache	Vitamin B6, niacinamide
	Tingling, numbness, burning skin	Vitamin B1, vitamin B2
	Low back pain	Folic acid, vitamin B12
	Lack of muscular co-ordination	Vitamin B1, vitamin B12
	Personality changes	Niacinamide
	Loss of memory	Vitamin B1, vitamin B12
		niacinamide, folic acid
	Muscle wasting and weakness	Vitamin B1, vitamin B6
	Loss of senses	Vitamin B1, vitamin B6
	Dragging of the feet (footdrop)	Vitamin B1
	Reduced tendon jerks	Vitamin B1
	Sub acute combined degeneration	
	of the spinal cord	Vitamin B12
	Stress	Vitamin B Complex,
		vitamin C, vitamin E
Skin	Haemorrhaging	Vitamin C, vitamin K
	Dry skin	Vitamin A
	Yellow coloration	Vitamin B12
	Hardening of the skin	Vitamin A
	Spiral and unerupted hairs	Vitamin C
	Genitalia dermatitis	Vitamin B2, niacinamide
	Burning feet	Pantothenic acid
	Pallor	Folic acid, vitamin B12
	Scar tissue	Vitamin E
	Pregnancy striae	Vitamin E
Eyes	Poor night vision	Vitamin A
	Dry eyes	Vitamin A, vitamin B2
	Blurred vision	Vitamin B1
	Bloodshot eyes	Vitamin B2
	Dim vision	Vitamin B1, niacinamide
	Intraocular haemorrhage	Vitamin C, vitamin K
	Optic neuritis	Vitamin B1, vitamin B12.

SUMMARY TABLE *continued*

Signs and Symptoms of Vitamin Deficiency

Affected Area	*Signs/Symptoms*	*Possible Vitamin Deficiency*
Lips, tongue and mouth	Inflammation	Vitamin B2
	Ulceration	Vitamin B2
	Fissures at corners of lips	Vitamin B2, vitamin B6
	Lips that hurt	Vitamin B1
	Sore tongue, inflamed tongue	Vitamin B12, vitamin B2, Niacinamide, folic acid Vitamin B6
	Beefy red swollen tongue	Niacinamide
	Fissured tongue	Vitamin B2
	Magenta-coloured	Vitamin B2
Gums	Bleeding and spongy	Vitamin C
	Gingivitis (inflamed)	Niacinamide
Face	Seborrhoea of nose and lips	Vitamin B2, vitamin B6
	Cheek pigmentation	Niacinamide
Skeletal system	Softening of the skull (babies)	Vitamin D
	Swelling of the skull (babies)	Vitamin D .
	Swelling of the joints (babies)	Vitamin D
	Painful bleeding of joints	Vitamin C
Gastrointestinal	Diarrhoea	Niacinamide
	Digestive disorders	Vitamin B1
	Paralytic ileus	Pantothenic acid
Blood	Anaemia	Folic acid, vitamin B12 vitamin C, vitamin B6
	Haemolytic anaemia	Vitamin E

3 | Medical Causes of Deficiency

As most of the vitamins are water-soluble they will tend to be eliminated in the watery excretion of the body such a sweat, tears and urine. When diarrhoea is present, the watery faeces may also contain excessive amounts of vitamins because, in this condition, absorption of vitamins is curtailed and hence more readily excreted. Losses through perspiration can be significant in excessive physical exertion, as in athletes, or as a result of living in hot climates. Tobacco smoke can inactivate vitamin C. Alcohol can cause excessive release of the B vitamins and vitamin C from the liver and hence from the body via the urine. Alcohol is also able to inhibit absorption of some vitamins from the food. These vitamin losses must be replaced by an improved diet or by supplementation with a multivitamin preparation.

INFECTIONS
Any sort of bacterial or viral infection can give rise to deficiencies of vitamins A and C. On the other hand, infections are more likely in those suffering from malnutrition and hence vitamin deficiency, particularly amongst children. Infections can aggravate malnutrition by reducing the appetite and, in turn, malnutrition weakens resistance to illness – a vicious circle indeed. The infections most likely to occur in malnourished children are bacterial (e.g. tuberculosis), viral (e.g. measles which can be a killing disease in malnutrition) and those due to parasites.

The ultimate result of vitamin A deficiency upon the eye is a condition called keratomalacia which induces blindness but is aggravated by any concurrent infections. Vitamin deficiency may lower resistance to infection by a reduced antibody formation; reduced activity of the white blood cells (phagocytes) which usually engulf invading bacteria and viruses; decrease the levels of protective enzymes (e.g. lysozyme, an enzyme in tears that protects the eyes); reduce the integrity of the skin and mucous membranes, the wet surfaces of the body, and so allowing invading micro-organisms to flourish. At one time vitamin A was referred to as 'the anti-infective vitamin' but now we know that all the vitamins, in one way or another, contribute to the body's resistance to disease.

Adequate intakes of the whole range will therefore contribute to the defences of the body.

Infections can precipitate gross deficiencies of vitamins in those on a poor diet and even mild deficiencies in those on an adequate diet. For example, children with meningitis, diarrhoea, tuberculosis, measles and other acute infections can develop vitamin deficiency severe enough to cause them to develop keratomalacia and, eventually, blindness. Glandular fever (infective mono-nucleosis) is notorious in inducing deficiency across the range of vitamins and supplementation with a high potency multivitamin preparation should be taken by those with this infection, particularly during the period of convalescence. All types of fever can cause symptoms of scurvy in children due to vitamin C deficiency, even when there appear to be adequate dietary intakes. Thiamine deficiency caused by fever can drop to such levels as to give rise to the symptoms of beriberi, the ultimate deficiency disease.

Infections often cause loss of appetite, so vitamin intake is much reduced and this is exacerbated by losses due to the infection. Hence supplementation during the period of convalescence following the illness is most important since even a return to a normal appetite is unlikely to rapidly make up the deficit of vitamins caused in the first place by the infection.

MALABSORPTION SYNDROMES

There are several clinical conditions which are characterised by an inability of the individual to absorb the micro nutrients in the diet. Most of these conditions result in fat malabsorption and since the fat soluble vitamins A, D, E and K are absorbed by the same mechanisms as dietary fats, they too are not absorbed or are absorbed only to a limited extent. Only one water-soluble vitamin B12, is affected by a malabsorption syndrome.

Impaired absorption of fats and fat soluble vitamins is a feature of the following diseases: sprue, idiopathic steatorrhoea, pancreatic disease, lack of bile production due to liver disease, gall bladder blockage and any disease affecting the production of fat-splitting digestive enzymes and bile salts. The latter are essential for emulsifying fats, a necessary prerequisite to their digestion and absorption.

Vitamin B12 may be present in adequate amounts in the diet but there are some conditions where it cannot be absorbed. The reason is that the vitamin is assimilated into the body by a unique mechanism. It must be complexed with a specific protein called intrinsic factor before absorption can take place. For some reason, certain people cease producing intrinsic factor and the resulting lack of B12 absorption gives rise to pernicious anaemia. Treatment of this condition can only be carried out successfully with intramuscular injections of the vitamin. It is, therefore, a matter of correct diagnosis of pernicious anaemia first, followed by medical treatment with injectable B12 and for these reasons therapy must be left to the medical practitioner.

MEDICINAL DRUGS

The common medicinal drugs, some of them available without prescription, may affect the nutritional status of the individual taking them. Some of these drugs increase the requirement for certain of the vitamins. For example, the synthetic oestrogens and progestogens in the contraceptive pill may increase the woman's need for vitamin B6. She must, therefore, take extra vitamin B6 to satisfy her requirements and often the quantity of the vitamin in her diet, even if this is highly nutritious, is not sufficient. It is essential for her, therefore, to take a vitamin B6 supplement, usually between 25 and 100mg daily.

Drugs may also interfere with the absorption of some vitamins so that when the medicine is taken with food the full nutritional benefit of that food is not obtained. Folic acid and vitamin B12, for example, are poorly absorbed in the presence of para-aminosalicylic acid (used to treat tuberculosis); phenytoin (a drug used to treat epilepsy) and colchicine (used to treat gout). There are however two important exceptions to this. First, when taking phenytoin, folic acid supplements should not be taken without medical advice. This is because excess folic acid may neutralise the beneficial effect of the drug. Second, extra vitamin B6 should not be taken with the drug levodopa (used in Parkinson's disease) because the vitamin interferes with the beneficial action of the drug.

Some drugs may interfere with the utilisation and activation of vitamins. The best example of this is the medicine liquid paraffin which has been widely used to act as an intestinal lubricant in cases of constipation. Liquid paraffin dissolves the fat-soluble vitamins present in the diet or in supplements and prevents them being absorbed. As liquid paraffin is neither digested nor absorbed, the vitamins become trapped within it and are no longer available for absorption through the intestinal system. The occasional use of liquid paraffin as an anti-constipation agent has no significant effect upon the fat-soluble vitamins, but when taken constantly, for example by the aged, the liquid paraffin may immobilise the fat-soluble vitamins to such an extent that deficiency is possible. The treatment is to take the fat soluble vitamins as supplements at a different time of day to that when liquid paraffin is taken. Alternatively, in really severe cases, the vitamins can be injected in order to bypass the intestine and the problems with liquid paraffin. Another way to overcome the problem is to take the fat-soluble vitamins in a water-solubilised form so that they are then not available for solution into the liquid paraffin. Typical daily supplements are between 2,500 and 7,500 i.u. vitamin A; 200 to 400 i.u. vitamin D and up to 250 i.u. vitamin E. Vitamin K should be taken at the discretion of a medical practitioner.

Aspirin is one of the most widely used analgesic drugs yet its effect upon vitamin C has been known since 1936. When aspirin was taken by children, the urinary excretion of vitamin C increased. Two aspirin tablets (600mg of the active drug acetylsalicylic acid) taken by healthy adults every six hours were found to result in a 100 per cent increase in the 24-hour excretion of ascorbic acid. An intake of aspirin such as this (2.4g or 8 aspirin tablets daily) is not unusual in the treatment of arthritic conditions, so anyone undertaking this therapy should be aware of a possible vitamin C deficiency.

A constant feature in arthritic patients is reduced levels of vitamin C in their white blood cells. As these cells act in the blood as scavengers of infective bacteria and viruses, and as their efficiency in this respect is dependent on adequate vitamin C levels, it is not surprising that many arthritis sufferers being treated with aspirin are prone to infections. Studies reported in *The Lancet* concluded that between 200 and 300mg of vitamin C should be swallowed with every two aspirin tablets.

There are other benefits to be gained from taking vitamin C with aspirin. Apart from simple replacement of the vitamin C lost, the vitamin also increases the efficacy of aspirin by increasing its absorption. This, in turn, leads to faster pain relief, a slower rate of excretion of the drug and longer duration of its action. The well-known side-effects of aspirin taken alone include gastric discomfort, blood loss, sedation and reduced vitamin C status. All of these reactions are reduced by taking extra vitamin C, but it must be eaten simultaneously with the drug. Studies reported in *The Lancet* in 1968 indicated that aspirin is more likely to cause gastric bleeding when vitamin C levels in the individual are low.

The conditions for which aspirin is taken, including the common cold, influenza, rheumatoid arthritis and osteoarthritis, themselves create a greater requirement for vitamin C. Treating such diseases with aspirin will therefore worsen the deficiency of the vitamin. Remember, too, that the ability of the body to fight off infections and to heal itself and reduce inflammation is very much dependent on a good supply of vitamin C. Aspirin may therefore be depleting the body of the very vitamin it needs for its own protection. Also remember that these effects of aspirin are shared to some extent by the non-steroidal anti-inflammatory drugs used to treat arthritis.

Corticosteroids (steroid drugs), used in medicine for a wide variety of diseases and conditions also induce excretion of vitamin C. In addition though, vitamin B6 is affected to such an extent that increased requirements are needed to maintain normal body levels. The mineral zinc is also excreted under the influence of corticosteroid drugs and this too should feature in the diet of those taking these drugs over prolonged periods. It is not without significance that anyone who is treated with corticosteroid drugs over any length of the time usually finds that any wounds they suffer will take a longer time to heal than in those who are not taking such drugs. We know that vitamin C and zinc are both essential to the healing of wounds so their excessive losses due to the steroid drugs may well be factors in determining a slow healing rate.

Administration of antibiotics, such as the tetracycline's, have been found to lower the level of vitamin C in the white blood cells and in the blood plasma. The reason is that the antibiotic appears to prevent the normal conservation of the vitamin by the kidneys so it is lost. The resulting white blood cell levels of vitamin C cause a reduced ability to resist infection. Hence patients, such as those with chronic bronchitis who are on prolonged regular treatment with antibiotics, are at risk of both an impaired vitamin C status and weakened natural defence mechanisms. The young should also be aware of this vitamin C-wasting effect of tetracycline antibiotics since low doses of them are often prescribed for very long periods in the treatment of acne. Vitamin C supplementation at levels up to 500mg daily becomes essential for anyone on long-term antibiotic treatment.

There is little doubt that antibiotics in general can have a deleterious effect upon the intestinal bacteria which under normal circumstances are useful providers of some of the B-vitamins and of vitamin K. Not only is the body deprived of these vitamins by the destruction caused by the antibiotics but replenishment of the friendly bacteria is curtailed as their normal balance is upset. Redressing the balance is best carried out by supplementing the diet with the B complex at fairly high potencies. At the same time, eating natural yoghurt is often recommended because it is a rich source of the friendly bacteria organisms. Taking the vitamin B complex with antibiotics and, indeed after the drug treatment has finished, will prevent the gastro-intestinal side-effects often associated with this type of therapy.

We have seen how various drugs most commonly used in medicine can upset the vitamin balance of the body. Replenishment with the vitamin is usually straightforward. There are, however, many other drugs that can affect vitamin status so extra vitamins are useful. Many treatments, of course, are short-term and perhaps in these cases any effect upon vitamins is transitory and so they tend to be ignored. You should be aware though of any prolonged medicinal therapy that can upset the nutritional basis of the body and protect yourself accordingly by taking the right supplements.

PARASITIC INFECTIONS

These include the various worm infections that can thrive in the intestinal tract. The worms utilise the vitamins in the diet before the micro nutrients can be absorbed, so a deficiency can be induced. The most likely vitamin to be affected is B12 because this is present in minute quantities anyway and parasitic worms have a particular affinity for this vitamin.

POOR DIGESTION

This condition can be a contributory factor in causing certain vitamin deficiencies. Digestive upsets can arise because of defective chewing of food; by a reduction in the volume and acidity of gastric secretions; by inefficient production of digestive enzymes in the pancreatic, liver and intestinal juices; by a reduction in bile secretion, affecting mainly the fat-soluble vitamins. When a meal is eaten, the vitamins are liberated only as the food is digested. Hence a defective digestion system will not allow the vitamins to be presented for absorption at the right spot in the intestinal tract and a slow, insidious deficiency may develop.

RAPID GROWTH

When a foetus is in the developing stage within the womb, all the vitamins are needed for its growth. These are supplied via the blood of the mother, so her dietary intakes of vitamins must satisfy her own needs as well as those of the developing baby. Once born, a child needs vitamins for its growth as well as for normal metabolism. Many animal studies have indicated that the offspring who do not have intakes of vitamins adequate for both purposes will suffer in their growth process. A similar situation applies also to the growing child whose vitamin intakes must be optimum rather than simply adequate. Most authorities agree that the need for vitamins in children is relatively higher than that in adults, when worked out on a body-weight or food-intake basis.

4 | Treating Yourself with Vitamins

There is no doubt that many factors can contribute to a mild and sometimes temporary deficiency of vitamins, sufficient in some people to cause ill-health and to prevent their living at one hundred per cent of their potential. Simple supplementation, often with a general all-round multivitamin preparation or, in the case of specific deficiencies, with the particular vitamin affected is usually enough to overcome problems associated with reduced intakes. When these are a result of poor diet, fairly low potencies of all the vitamins are usually sufficient to insure against any deficiency. However, when the factors inducing deficiency are associated with life styles, medicinal drugs and habits like smoking and drinking, rather higher potencies of the missing vitamins may be needed up to five or even ten times the recommended minimum daily allowances. To these two groups must now be added a third, that of high potency intakes where the vitamin or vitamins are being used for their therapeutic effect in certain clinical conditions.

When the vitamin intake has reached such a low degree that a gross deficiency disease (such as, for example, beriberi, pellagra or scurvy, due respectively to lack of thiamine, nicotinic acid or vitamin C) manifests itself, then diagnosis and treatment become the province of the medical practitioner. Such diseases are rare in this country and in the Western world in general but occasionally they do appear. The symptoms of beriberi, for example, are not uncommon in alcoholics, but when deficiency has reached this stage, it is not suitable for self-treatment and professional help must be sought. This is not to say that anyone who drinks alcohol regularly should not be aware that their vitamin B complex (particularly thiamine) status is at risk, but if they are, regular supplementation with these vitamins, plus vitamin C, should at least ensure that they are unlikely to reach the stage of alcoholic beriberi. In fact, it has been seriously suggested that vitamin B1 should be added to alcoholic drinks to help those who will not help themselves. There is also some evidence that high intakes of the vitamin B complex and vitamin C can help remove the craving for alcohol in chronic alcoholics.

What we are more concerned with in this book is how people who wish to treat themselves with vitamins at high dose can do so safely and successfully. Vitamins will often complement medicinal drug treatments but therapy with these micro nutrients should never be used as a replacement for prescribed drugs without the full knowledge of the doctor prescribing those drugs. Vitamins will not interfere with medicines, with one or two exceptions already noted previously, and indeed both will often function effectively together. You may rest assured, therefore, that the dosage regimes suggested are safe and in the trials where they have been tested, are beneficial. Trials can vary in the way they are carried out but it is accepted that the most meaningful trial is known as double-blind. A double-blind trial compares the effect of the vitamin with a harmless compound (placebo) in a similar presentation in the treatment of the condition. Double-blind simply means that neither the patient nor doctor knows which is which until the end of the trial. In this way the result cannot be influenced by personal bias.

Cancer

VITAMIN A

There are few instances of vitamin A or beta-carotene therapy actually curing an established cancer (a prescribable derivative called retinoic acid has helped in skin cancer) but there are many studies indicating a correlation between body levels of the vitamins and the chances of developing cancer. When blood levels of vitamin A and/or beta-carotene are persistently low, the incidence of cancer increases. This was first illustrated in animal experiments when it was noted that apparently healthy animals which had low body levels of vitamin A were more susceptible to the formation of tumours than those with adequate levels of the vitamin.

Observations on humans have also suggested that low vitamin A or beta-carotene intakes may increase their susceptibility to cancer. Typical is a five-year follow-up study of 8,278 men in Norway. Here, the incidence of confirmed lung cancer and glandular cancers was 4.6 times higher in men classified as having low vitamin A intake. This difference was statistically highly significant and independent of smoking habits. Other studies of blood vitamin A levels, measured as retinol, have demonstrated lower levels in patients with cancer than in control persons without cancer.

A survey, starting in 1975, was carried out as a joint study between Radcliffe Infirmary, Oxford and BUPA Medical Research and reported in *The Lancet* (1980). In a prospective study of about 16,000 men who attended the BUPA Medical Centre for health screening, blood samples were collected and stored at deep freeze temperatures. By the end of 1979, 86 men were identified who had developed cancer. Another 172 men who were alive and without cancer were selected from the remainder of the study population as a control group for comparison. The men in this group were chosen because of similar age and similar smoking habits and because their blood was taken at almost identical times. Vitamin A levels were measured as well as other criteria, such as blood cholesterol. What emerged from the study was that low vitamin A levels were associated with an increased risk of cancer. This association was independent of age, smoking habits and serum cholesterol levels and was greatest for men who developed lung cancer. Their vitamin A levels were only 18 i.u. per 100ml of blood compared with 229 i.uc. per 100ml for the men in control group. The risk of cancer at any body site for men with retinol levels at the lower end of the scale was 2.2. times greater than for those with the higher levels. The conclusion reached was that measures taken to increase serum vitamin A levels in men may lead to a reduction in cancer risk.

A comparable study was carried out on 3,100 patients in Evans County, Georgia in the USA. Low blood levels of vitamin A proved to be associated with an increased incidence of cancer that was independent of age and smoking habits. It was further found that those people who died of lung cancer invariably had lower blood levels not only of vitamin A, but of beta-carotene also, compared to those dying of non-cancer diseases. In these cases, it was also possible to measure the vitamin and its precursor in the liver, and again it was found that reserves of both nutrients were much lower in the cancer victims.

When we look at the relationship between a specific type of tumour, namely lung cancer, and vitamin A intake and smoking habits, a more significant connection emerges. Dr. E. Bjelke reported, in the *International Journal of Cancer*, that when men were matched for equivalent tobacco smoking habits, those with a lower dietary intake of vitamin A had a higher incidence of lung cancer. The main dietary differences between the two groups was a higher consumption of carrots, milk and eggs in those people less prone to lung cancer. All these foods, of course, are excellent sources of vitamin A and carotene. However, other findings emerged from the results. Dietary vitamin A was found to be inversely related to a five year risk of lung cancer among men who were current or former cigarette smokers. After allowing for the number of cigarettes smoked per day, men with lower levels of blood vitamin A, who also ate less quantities of vitamin A and beta carotene-rich foods, had more than 2.5 times the chance of developing lung cancer than those with good intakes of these micro nutrients.

Confirmation that beta-carotene appears to confer a better protective effect against lung cancer than vitamin A was suggested by a study carried out on employees of the Western Electric Company in Chicago, USA. A total of 2,107 men were examined in October 1957 and December 1958 as to their dietary habits, including the taking of vitamin supplements. All the men participating in the trial were re-examined in this manner annually until 1969. Nine years after this the incidence of cancer over the 19 years following the start of the trial was assessed. The results were as follows. Men in the group that comprised the lowest 25 per cent of carotene intake had seven times the relative risk of lung cancer as men in the group that made up the highest 25 per cent of carotene intake. Among men who had smoked cigarettes for 30 years or more, the relative risk of developing lung cancer was eight times as great for men with low carotene consumption as for those with a high intake of the pro-vitamin.

After analysis of other nutrients in the diet, the authors of the study concluded that the key dietary variable related to risk of lung cancer is carotene. Pre-formed vitamin A and other nutrients provided by their diets were not significantly related to the risk of lung cancer.

The authors conclude that a diet relatively high in beta-carotene may reduce the risk of lung cancer, even among persons who have smoked cigarettes for many years. They emphasise, however, that cigarette smoking increases the risk of other serious diseases such as strokes and coronary thrombosis and there is no evidence that dietary carotene affects the chances of developing these.

Similarly, studies from Israel reported in the *International Journal of Cancer* indicate that there is no protective effect of vitamin A consumption against cancers of the gastro-intestinal tract, but there is a decreased risk of cancer in those who eat beta-carotene rich foods.

We can conclude, therefore, that beta-carotene is preferred to vitamin A as a natural dietary agent to protect against cancer. Even in those with cancer, it is advisable to take extra beta-carotene (13.5mg daily) which may slow down the growth of the cancer. As beta-carotene is much less toxic than vitamin A, the amount suggested will do no harm. It is perhaps significant that fruit and vegetables, both rich in beta-carotene, appear to protect the individual against cancers of the stomach and of the colon.

VITAMIN C

Many studies have found that the lower the amount of vitamin C eaten, the greater the chance of developing cancer. One study in Canada indicated that those with higher regular vitamin C intake in their diets had only 40 per cent of the incidences of those with persistently low intake of the vitamin in the same age groups. By increasing the daily intake of dietary vitamin C from 25mg to 125mg there was a 60 per cent decrease in the chances of developing cancer. This represents an increase of life expectancy of eleven years. At the same time, it has been observed that cancer sufferers usually have low body levels of vitamin C and their requirements are higher than those not suffering from the disease. The moral would therefore appear to be – ensure an optimal intake of vitamin C daily (say 500-1,000mg) and you could cut down your chance of developing cancer.

Actual therapy with vitamin C in treating cancers has been tried with varying results. Two typical studies are as follows:

Ascorbic acid has been shown to be effective against some artificially produced cancers in mice, rats and guinea-pigs but there are very few clinical trials in man. The most comprehensive was that reported by Dr. Ewan Cameron from the Vale of Leven Hospital in Scotland. He treated 100 advanced cancer patients with 10g of ascorbic acid per day (given as sodium ascorbate), and reported that they felt better, had more energy, had better appetites and, in some cases, suffered much less pain. In a few cases their tumours shrank, and in a very small proportion the growth disappeared. The most promising result was an increased average survival time of 293 days. a similar group of advanced cancer patients, who had not received vitamin C treatment had an average survival time of only 38 days. The results, though not outstanding, were promising. A similar study was therefore undertaken by the Mayo Clinic in Rochester, Minnesota, USA. These researchers reported in the New England Journal of Medicine that they had treated 60 advanced cancer patients with 10g of vitamin C per day, given as 20 tablets of 500mg each. A comparative group of 63 patients of the same type and stage of cancer, age and sex were given milk sugar tablets to act as a placebo, i.e. an innocuous substance that can have no therapeutic action. There was no difference in survival time of the two groups. About 80 per cent of the patients in each group were dead three months after the study began. All but one of the 123 patients were dead within eight months and the one left alive was taking placebo tablets. Even the improvements in symptoms were similar, 63 per cent of this category taking vitamin C and 58 per cent on milk sugar tablets.

The main difference between the two trials was that the patients in Scotland had not received the strong immunosuppressive drugs that those in USA had been treated with. Dr. Linus Pauling believes this may explain the different responses. He believes that the natural response of the body to vitamin C is weakened by the powerful drugs used in the North American study, most of which reduce the body's natural immunity. The fact remains, however, that in any type of cancer, but particularly those where the local concentration of vitamin C can be high, e.g. gastro intestinal and urinary system cancers, high doses of vitamin C are worth trying. The rule is to take one gram of the vitamin on the first day, two grams on the second and so on up to a maximum of ten grams daily. If the vitamin causes diarrhoea at any level, that potency less one gram should be the dose that is maintained daily. Using this technique it is possible to arrive at one's tolerable level of vitamin C for taking on a regular basis.

LAETRILE

This substance, incorrectly called vitamin B17, is extracted from apricot kernels and it has been claimed to be of benefit in treating various cancers. It contains organic cyanide which is believed by its proponents to act against the tumour, causing its regression. Unfortunately, it is possible to take too much laetrile which can give rise to cyanide poisoning. For this reason the substance has now been put on the prescription-only list in the UK so it is not suitable for self-treatment.

Skin Diseases

VITAMIN A

The skin-protecting properties of vitamin A are well established but when it was tried in high doses in acne, rosacea and psoriasis, its success rate was variable. At the same time, there were worries about possible side-effects from the megadoses used. In one trial, 18 patients were given up to 200,000 i.e. per day for between 15 and 20 injections. This course was repeated three or five times and the results were promising. Symptoms disappeared in seven patients, improved substantially in nine and improved slightly in two, but side-effects appeared and their extent was such as to cause cessation of the trial after a few months. However, trials such as these did give benefit to some sufferers from skin disease, so research was switched away from vitamin A itself to derivatives with similar or greater positive action but less side-effects. These include retinoic acid but this is not available on general sale.

There are many anecdotal reports of the benefits of relatively low-dose supplementation of vitamin A, (i.e. up to 10,000 i.u. daily) on acne, eczema and psoriasis and other skin complaints. The action of vitamin A is enhanced by simultaneous supplementation with the mineral zinc (up to 15mg daily) probably because one function of this mineral is to ensure adequate uptake of the vitamin by tissues and its release from the liver.

Since acne often appears during puberty, it has been suggested that the sex hormones are involved in its development. We know that vitamin A is necessary for the natural production of sex hormones so it may be acting through these. Whatever the mechanism however, this low dose regime of vitamin A plus zinc has been successful in relieving minor skin complaints in some people.

OIL OF EVENING PRIMROSE

The oil of the Evening Primrose is another natural product claimed to help in clearing up mild skin complaints when taken at the rate of 750 mg daily. The mode of action of this oil is to supply precursors of other important body hormones known as prostaglandins. These, too, may have a role to play in normalizing skin cell formation and again their action may be activated through vitamin A and zinc. The sensible way to approach self-treatment of these skin complaints is to ensure there is no deficiency of any of these factors. Supplementation at the levels recommended will do this, and it is comforting to know that there is no harm at these potencies. In addition, if you can obtain some Oil of Evening Primrose Cream or ointment, this can be applied directly to the skin lesions and so increase the effect of the oral treatment.

BIOTIN

This member of the vitamin B complex can be used in some cases of scaly dermatitis. It is of particular benefit in babies who develop seborrhoeic dermatitis – a dry scaling of the scalp and face. This is sometimes associated with breast-feeding as human milk is low in biotin. Up to 10mg daily will cure this condition but similar doses are worth trying in other cases of scaly dermatitis. Other skin complaints, alopecia and scalp conditions may also respond to these intakes of biotin which are perfectly safe to take.

Ulcers

VITAMIN B2

Recurrent mouth ulcers have been claimed to be prevented by daily intakes of 20mg or more of vitamin B2. Similar studies on stomach and duodenal ulcers resulted in a less dramatic response, but this was probably because these lesions are a result of many factors, amongst which may be riboflavin deficiency.

Ulceration of the cornea of the eye will sometimes respond to high potency supplementation with vitamin B2. In a study of 47 patients suffering from eye and eyesight problems, six of whom were affected by cataracts, Dr. U. P. Sydenstricker reported in *Prevention* that all disorders were gradually cured with vitamin B2 supplementation. It was essential to carry on with the high riboflavin intake since, when this ceased, the eye complaints returned.

These results parallel those in animals suffering from this condition, but it must be stressed that other B vitamins, like pantothenic acid, may also be involved in prevention of cataracts. Recent research has equated low levels of vitamin C intake throughout life with increased chances of developing cataracts in later life.

VITAMIN A

Vitamin A has a protective effect on mucosal tissue, so it may have the potential for exerting a similar action against gastric ulcer. This hypothesis has been tested in a multi-centre, randomised, controlled trial of vitamin A in 60 patients with chronic gastric ulcers. The trial took place in Hungary and was reported in *The Lancet* towards the end of 1982.

There were three groups of patients. One group was treated only with antacids; the second group received similar antacids plus 150,000 i.u. of vitamin A; the third group were given the same doses of antacids and vitamin A as the second group but with the addition of the drug cyproheptadine.

All patients were treated for four weeks. Ulcer sizes were measured before and after treatment in each case.

Ulcers were all reduced to a significant degree, but the patients receiving vitamin A experienced a significantly greater reduction than those treated just with antacids. The authors concluded that 'a beneficial effect of vitamin A has been indicated in the prevention and treatment of stress ulcer in patients'.

Gastric ulcer can be thought of as a pre-cancerous state, and significant negative connection has been reported between low serum levels of vitamin A and the greater chance of development of lung, urinary, bladder and skin cancers. The results of this trial indicate a possible role for vitamin A in gastric protection by the prevention of the development of cancer from gastric ulcer!

Although the doses of vitamin A used are far beyond those acceptable for self-treatment, a daily supplementary intake of say 7,500 i.u. may be of benefit in those who have suffered from gastric and duodenal ulcers and wish to reduce the chances of others recurring. It may also help those with active ulcers to speed up their healing rate and protect them from further complications of their complaint.

VITAMIN E

Leg ulcers

Some leg ulcers are very resistant to conventional medical treatment and they often persist for long periods. They are prone to infection and cause a severe, burning and aching pain. Despite some 60 publications in medical journals on the effectiveness of vitamin E ointment for treating them, these ulcers are still a big problem for many people. They are associated with a poor blood supply to the limb, caused usually by varicose veins.

Application of the ointment and oral supplementation of the vitamin in the diet are usually sufficient to heal these ulcers. There is a word of caution from the proponents of this treatment, however. Once the ulcer has gone, oral supplementation of vitamin E should continue. This maintains local tissue oxygenation and blood circulation and prevents the ulcers from recurring.

Skin conditions, like acne and eczema, have responded to topical treatment with vitamin E ointment. There are many cases on record where multiple lacerations to the face as received in car accidents are completely and clearly healed up with combined topical and oral vitamin E treatment. Many surgery units now use vitamin E ointment routinely after operations. It reduces toxic reactions, then soothes and heals the irritated area. A dose suitable for oral treatment is 400 i.u. vitamin E once daily, or two 250 i.u. capsules twice daily. This intake is perfectly safe when taken over the prolonged periods that may be needed, treating skin diseases as well as scars that have been left behind after accidents or surgery. A similar regime may help remove the stretch marks (striae) left behind after childbirth or some drug treatments.

Arthritis

PANTOTHENIC ACID

Young rats deprived of pantothenic acid developed joint inflammation and the hardening of their bones was impaired. Pigs and dogs·were found to develop arthritic symptoms when pantothenic acid was missing from their diets.

A significant report then appeared in *The Lancet* regarding the blood pantothenic acid levels of various groups of people, with and without arthritis. What emerged was that the vegetarian group had significantly higher blood levels of pantothenic acid than those on a meat-eating diet.

The common factor in those suffering from arthritis, whether they were vegetarian or not, was the greatly reduced levels of pantothenic acid in their blood. In fact, the lower the level of pantothenic acid in the blood, the more severe were the symptoms of arthritis.

The two authors, Drs. E. C. Barton-Wright and W. A. Elliott then proceeded to test their hypothesis that rheumatoid arthritis is a vitamin-deficiency disease by treating arthritic patients with daily injections of 50mg calcium pantothenate. Within seven days, the blood levels of the vitamin increased and this was parallel by alleviation of the arthritic symptoms. This improvement persisted after further treatment for three weeks. However, discontinuing the supplementary calcium pantothenate caused the symptoms to return. Another report in the same journal from Dr. J. C. Annand claimed a similar result with the more difficult to treat serious disorder of osteo-arthritis.

These encouraging results led to a much larger trial of the vitamin in arthritis, organised by the General Practitioner Research Group and reported in *The Practitioner*. A total of 94 patients were involved and neither they nor the doctors knew whether the treatment was calcium pantothenate or a harmless placebo. Response to the treatment was assessed both by doctor and patient using a number of criteria. The dosage regime used was 500mg (1 tablet) daily for 2 days, 1,000mg (2 tablets) for 3 days, 1,500mg (3 tablets) for 4 days and finally 2,000mg (4 tablets) per day thereafter for a period of 2 months. Highly significant effects were recorded for calcium pantothenate in reducing the duration of morning stiffness, the degree of disability and the severity of pain.

Only in the condition of rheumatoid arthritis, however, was there any indication of a beneficial effect – there was little if any in the other types of arthritis. Why pantothenic acid should have this beneficial effect is not known with certainty, but an important clue lies in its function in controlling the synthesis of the anti-stress hormones of the body. Lack of the vitamin means lowered production of these hormones with subsequent development of inflammatory and degenerative diseases like arthritis. The ultimate treatment for these diseases consists of highly potent synthetic hormones known as corticosteroids. Pantothenic acid may enable the glands of the body to produce its own natural corticosteroids, so the end effect of either treatment is probably the same, but the vitamin therapy, of course, is far safer.

Reducing blood cholesterol

It is now generally believed that a high blood level of cholesterol increases the chances of fat deposition on the walls of blood vessels giving rise to the condition of atherosclerosis. The formation of a thrombus and hardening of the arteries (called arteriosclerosis) may also be more likely in those with high blood cholesterol levels. These high concentrations in the blood may also give rise to or be a consequence of excessive cholesterol in the bile which in turn predisposes to gall stone formation. Dietary measures to keep blood cholesterol in the normal range are now recommended as a general aid to good health. Vitamins taken at high doses may also contribute to control of cholesterol when this is high. What they will not do is reduce it below normal concentration.

NICOTINIC ACID

Nicotinic acid, but not nicotinamide, will reduce cholesterol levels in the blood. In a short term trial at the Mayo Clinic in the USA, 3g of nicotinic acid were given orally to patients with high blood cholesterol and levels were lowered to normal in 72 per cent of those tested. The remaining 28 per cent responded favourably to 4–6g per day. A longer term study over 11 years was carried out at the Dartmouth-Hitchcock Medical Centre in New Hampshire. A dose of 100mg nicotinic acid was given to 160 patients after each meal and this was increased over 11 days to 1g after each meal, at which level therapy continued. The average decrease in plasma cholesterol was 26 per cent in those who took the vitamin for at least a year, and the lower cholesterol level was maintained for as long as treatment continued. It was particularly gratifying to note that there were no serious side-effects.

Other studies in Britain have indicated that nicotinic acid also has the property of lowering blood fats (triglycerides) in general at the above doses. In this respect it appears to be as effective as the drug clofibrate. It is believed to act in two ways; first, by inhibiting the synthesis of fats in the blood; and second, by competing with and preventing the release of free fatty acids which combine with cholesterol. These high potencies of nicotinic acid may not always be available so other means to reduce cholesterol may have to be sought. There is always the possibility too that this vitamin (but not nicotinamide) may cause transient flushing in some individuals. In either case, you may wish to control your blood cholesterol by other means.

VITAMIN C

Guinea-pigs, like man, require a dietary source of vitamin C and when deprived of the vitamin they show increased blood levels of cholesterol and fats are deposited in the walls of blood vessels of the heart and brain. They also show a greater tendency to produce gall-stones.

These and similar studies on human beings have been carried out by Dr. E. Ginter of Czechoslovakia. He found that diabetic patients (who usually have high blood cholesterol) and others with similar high levels responded to 500mg vitamin C daily.

The blood cholesterol level and the total fat in the blood were reduced in all cases. This reduction was maintained while those patients were given ample vitamin C. Similar supplementation on a group of patients who did not have high cholesterol levels had no effect. In other words, ascorbic acid will reduce excessive cholesterol, but once normal levels are achieved it has no further influence.

How does vitamin C achieve cholesterol reduction? It increases the rate at which cholesterol is converted into bile acids and hence excreted. In his patients Dr. Ginter found no evidence of a higher excretion of cholesterol as such, but what did increase dramatically was their excretion of bile acids. The usual route through which the body disposes of cholesterol is to convert it into bile acids in the liver, which are then deposited in the bile, carried to the intestine where they assist in fat digestion and end up excreted in the faeces. Speeding up this process disposes of excess cholesterol. Drugs that decrease cholesterol usually do so by preventing its synthesis by the body. Recently, however, these drugs have received adverse publicity because of their serious side-effects. It looks now as though we have in vitamin C a safe, effective treatment that works in a more logical manner, by accelerating the disposal of cholesterol. Blood fats are also reduced by vitamin C, but although the mechanism is not completely worked out, the vitamin is just as effective and safe.

In addition, there may be other benefits from an intake of 500mg of ascorbic acid daily. Dr. Geoffrey Taylor, formerly professor of medicine at the University of Lahore, has reported that changes in the tiny blood vessels, particularly those under the tongue, may be the warning signs of impending stroke. These changes also appear in scurvy and in mild deficiency of vitamin C. The number of deaths from strokes and coronary heart disease increases in cold weather in the winter, when the need for ascorbic acid is highest, but intake is at its lowest. Dr. Constance Lesley of the Wakefield Group of Hospitals in Yorkshire is another expert who has found that vitamin C exerts a powerful protective on certain high risk groups of the population. It may play a role in preventing heart attacks, strokes, deep vein thrombosis and atherosclerosis through its cholesterol and fat-controlling mechanisms. All of these conditions are less prevalent in vegetarians and this may reflect their higher dietary vitamin C intake.

VITAMIN E

We hear a lot of how high blood cholesterol levels can be a factor in the development of certain diseases but recent research suggests that total blood cholesterol is not the complete answer – we should also be looking at the types of cholesterol in the body. Cholesterol is carried on the backs of various proteins which are called VLDL (Very Low Density Lipoprotein); LDL (Low Density Lipoprotein); HDL (High Density Lipoprotein). The balance of these is important and when LDL and VLDL predominate, the chances of problems arising are increased. Therapy at reducing blood cholesterol is also additionally aimed at increasing the desirable HDL. Vitamin E appears to do just that.

Vitamin E can influence the cholesterol metabolism in two ways. First it has been shown that in some cases it can actually decrease cholesterol levels. Second, it can influence the proportion of the various lipoproteins in the blood in favour of the desirable HDL. In both functions, animal experiments using rabbits, which are partially susceptible in atherosclerosis, have confirmed the beneficial action of vitamin E.

A report in the *Journal of Nutrition* is typical. Rabbits were fed an atherosclerosis-producing diet consisting of high butter intakes. There were three groups of animals on the diet; one group received supplementary vitamin E (the equivalent of a human adult receiving 400 i.u. daily); another group were fed BHA (butylated hydroxyanisole), a synthetic antioxidant much used in food and drugs; the third group were fed just the basic diet. After three years on the diets, there were significantly less frequent and less excessive atherosclerotic lesions in the aorta of those rabbits fed supplementary vitamin E than in the other two groups. Lower blood cholesterol levels were noted in the vitamin E group and it was this that was considered to be the main factor in inhibiting atherosclerosis.

Studies confirming that vitamin E can also reduce blood cholesterol levels in human beings were reported by Drs. M. Passeri and U. Butturini of the University of Parma, Italy in an International Symposium in Madrid. It was pointed out, however, that although this beneficial effect was related to a daily intake of 300 to 400 i.u. of vitamin F, extra vitamins A and C were more effective.

Other studies have indicated that 600 i.u. vitamin E taken for 30 days increased the proportion of HDL cholesterol from 9 per cent to 40 per cent. If the LDL cholesterol is high, the increase in HDL cholesterol is even more dramatic, up to 200 percent. In all cases blood cholesterol levels were normal; vitamin E simply shifted the balance to the more desirable HDL cholesterol.

Respiratory infections

VITAMIN C AND THE COMMON COLD

Controversy over whether vitamin C taken in large doses can prevent or help relieve the symptoms of the common cold and other respiratory infections still rages but it now looks as if the trials confirming its benefits are outweighing those which were claimed to be negative. One reason is that daily intakes of the vitamins must be high to confer benefit; in many of the trials giving negative results they were carried out using relatively low doses.

Accordingly, a carefully controlled study with the relatively large amount of 1,000mg vitamin C was carried out by Dr. G. Ritzel of Switzerland. All of the 279 subjects were boys of similar age (16 to 17 years) and there were two periods of study, namely five and seven days. Neither investigators nor the boys knew whether they were taking their gram of ascorbic acid per day or a harmless placebo, so the trial was truly double-blind. The boys were examined daily by medical methods, for symptoms of colds and other infections and were also assessed on their own judgement symptoms. There was no doubt in this trial that vitamin C at the level given was of benefit in preventing and treating colds. Of the 140 subjects receiving placebo, 31 developed colds as against 17 out of 139 of those receiving 1,000mg of vitamin C. Moreover, the duration of the colds was some 29 per cent less in the treated boys than those on placebo tablets.

A similar double-blind trial involving 641 children in a Navajo boarding school gave comparable results. Dr. J. L. Coulehan and his colleagues reported in the *New England Journal of Medicine* (1974), that giving 321 children 1g or 2g of ascorbic acid per day over 14 weeks reduced the average number of days with colds by 30 per cent over a similar number of children not treated. They benefited in other ways too; in total there was 17 per cent less time off sick, involving diseases other than those of the respiratory tract.

The most comprehensive and well-organised controlled trials were carried out in Toronto, Canada and reported in the *Canadian Medical Association Journal* by Dr. T. W. Anderson and colleagues. The dosage regime varied slightly but the general conclusion was that 500 to 1,000mg vitamin C taken daily was a good preventative dose. If cold symptoms did develop, three grams per day was usually sufficient to reduce them. All subjects were assessed for their symptoms of respiratory disease and for their mental attitude. The investigators concluded that subjects in vitamin-treated groups experienced less severe illness than subjects not given vitamin C with approximately 25 per cent fewer days spent indoors because of illness.

The longest and most successful clinical trial on record is that carried out by Dr. Edine Reginier of Massachusetts, USA, and report in the *Review of Allergy*. He treated 22 patients for five years, using the following regime: 600mg ascorbic acid at the first sign of a cold followed by 600mg every three hours, or 200mg every hour. At bedtime the amount taken was increased to 750mg. This quantity (4g per day) was continued for three or four days then reduced to 400mg every three hours for several days, further reducing to 200mg every three hours. With this regime, the vitamin C taken had bioflavonoids in addition, and of 34 colds, 31 were averted.

Excellent results were also obtained with vitamin C alone when 45 out of 50 colds were averted. This method of taking vitamin C at the onset of a cold is a sensible one and it avoids the sudden discontinuation of the vitamin that was a feature of less successful trials.

Mental Conditions

MILD DEPRESSION: PYRIXODINE AND L-TRYPTOPHANE

A nerve substance called serotonin is produced constantly in the brain and at nerve endings. When it is not, serotonin levels drop and the results are a form of depression and sleep disturbance. The control of mood is dependent on brain concentrations of serotonin whose synthesis depends on two important food constituents, pyridoxine (vitamin B6) and the amino acid l-tryptophane. Lack of either of these will give similar symptoms to those when serotonin synthesis is reduced. Hence both or either may be used to overcome mild depression and to induce sleep.

We have seen already how a women taking the contraceptive pill may develop mild depression because the constituents of the pill increase her requirements for vitamin B6. Similarly, even when not taking this form of contraception, a woman's needs for the vitamin can increase ten days or so before menstruation. In both cases the natural approach is to take 100mg daily of vitamin B6 for ten days before menstruation or to take 25 to 50mg of the vitamin daily from day ten of one cycle to day three of the next.

Sleep disturbances may be treated with the amino acid-l-tryptophane if 500mg or 1,000mg of this is taken just before going to bed, but remember that this amino acid can only be prescribed by a medical practitioner. It is not recommended that greater doses of this should be taken, nor should the amino acid be taken during the day at this level since drowsiness may be induced. L-tryptophane at much higher doses can be prescribed for certain types of depression but this therapy should be under the supervision of a medical practitioner.

SCHIZOPHRENIA: NICOTINIC ACID AND NICOTINAMIDE

The mental symptoms associated with subclinical or mild pellagra are similar to those seen in schizophrenia and include tension, depression, personality problems and mental fatigue. These observations led Drs. H. Osmond and A. Hoffer of the University of Saskatchewan in Canada to suggest that this particular mental disease may respond to nicotinic acid in the same way as those who suffer from pellagra.

Accordingly, these doctors treated their first schizophrenic patients with high doses (3g to 6g) of the vitamin and reported dramatic results. They postulated that these patients had a biochemical abnormality that demanded a higher than usual intake of nicotinic acid so that even a good diet, supplying enough of the vitamin for the usual individual, was not sufficient. It was also suggested that a normal dietary intake of nicotinic acid could lead to a localized deficiency of the vitamin in the brains of these people. Although there was sufficient nicotinic acid to prevent the other symptoms of deficiency affecting the skin and digestive system it was believed that there was an abnormal barrier to the vitamin between the blood and brain in schizophrenia so that the brain was ostensibly starved of the vitamin.

Since these early successes, many doctors have reported similar results and clinics devoted to what is termed mega vitamin therapy have been founded. One such clinic is in New York where Dr. D. Hawkins has treated more than 4,000 patients with high doses of nicotinic acid. Where the acid cannot be tolerated at high levels, the neutral nicotinamide may be used. Sometimes better results were obtained when vitamin C was given at the same time. Doses of 4g each of nicotinic acid and vitamin C were required daily in some cases, with occasionally 50mg of vitamin B6. Dr. A. Cott reported in the journal Schizophrenia that it was also possible to administer high doses of these vitamins by injection in acute cases of the disease, but oral treatment could continue for several years.

No one should attempt self-treatment with these massive doses since each individual requires different amounts that depend upon personal requirements as well as upon any other treatments utilizing drugs. It must also be said there are clinical studies on record where no response was obtained when treating schizophrenics with nicotinic acid. Dr. C. C. Pfieffer, Chairman of the Brain Biocentre at Princeton, New Jersey believes that schizophrenic patients who have a high level of histamine in their bodies are less likely to respond to megadose nicotinic acid, and this may explain the varying responses to mega vitamin therapy.

Schizophrenic children may also respond to high doses of nicotinic acid or nicotinamide. Three grams of the vitamin, plus 500mg of vitamin B6 daily were reported by Dr. A. Hoffer to be of value in treating them and also hyperactive children. Those with poor learning ability often responded to 1–2g of nicotinic acid daily with the addition of the same amount of vitamin C, plus 200–400mg of vitamin B6. Dr. A. Cott believes that the reason for many of these mental diseases associated with childhood lies partly in an unbalanced diet high in refined foods plus an unusual demand for certain vitamins because of some biochemical abnormality. This is why they will respond only to doses far above those in the diet. Such doses can only be given under the supervision of a medical practitioner.

Mental Ability

THIAMINE

When we consider how essential thiamine is to nerve and brain function, it is perhaps not surprising that the vitamin appears to improve mental ability. In a study of children aged 9 to 19 years, Dr. R. F. Harvell of Columbia University compared the effect of supplementation on one group, with the relatively low level of 2mg thiamine per day, with an unsupplemented group. Diets in both groups were identical and thought to be adequate. After one year there was a large increase in the mental achievements of those receiving the extra vitamin using the criteria of mental alertness, emotional stability, lack of depression and zest for life. Neither group at any time showed symptoms of B1 deficiency suggesting that the added vitamin was exerting an effect over and above that of the norm.

FOLIC ACID

A study from Masschusetts General Hospital, reported in the *New England Journal of Medicine* revealed that some mentally disturbed or retarded patients responded favourably to folic acid treatment. Even schizophrenics lose some of their psychotic symptoms. It has been mentioned previously that vitamin B6 is necessary in the production of certain chemicals that are normally released at nerve ending and folic acid too plays a part in the process. Certainly, in the above-mentioned study, it was found that both vitamin B6 and folic acid were essential in overcoming the mental symptoms. Neither was effective alone. Yet reports from Northwick Park Hospital, Middlesex have indicated that schizophrenia and other mental conditions have benefited from folic acid alone. What it agreed, however, is that some mental problems will respond to folic acid and at doses of only between 5mg and 20mg per day which must be taken under medical supervision..

VITAMIN B12

The knowledge that vitamin B12 deficiency produces nerve degeneration has stimulated studies into its use in brain and nerve disturbances. Old people with mild mental problems often respond to the vitamin. Dr. O. Abransky of the Hadassah University Medical School of Jerusalem has treated many old people who exhibited mental apathy, moodiness, poor memory, paranoia and confusion with vitamin B12 injections, bringing excellent results. A consultant psychiatrist at the University of Aberdeen Dr. J. G. Handerson, has reported similar benefits in old people and believes that 'Vitamin B12 deficiency may be a possible diagnosis in the majority of psychiatric patients'. Mental disorders due to B12 deficiency are not confined to the old, and younger people often benefit from treatment with the vitamin. The fact that mental symptoms often appear before the anaemia associated with B12 deficiency would suggest that in these cases the patient's B12 level should be first examined. This is particularly so when an adequate intake of the vitamin from the food is in question.

CHOLINE

Choline, in the form of a simple derivative called acetylcholine, is essential in transmitting nerve impulses. Although nerves may be thought of as power cables - vehicles for carrying electric impulses – the resemblance ends where the nerve meets another nerve or the muscle it is controlling. Here electrical energy causes acetylcholine, which is stored in the nerve ending, to be released and in so doing it relays the message to the next nerve or to the muscle causing it to react. To prevent the acetylcholine from having a continuous action on the muscle, it is inactivated very quickly, allowing the muscle to relax and await the next nerve impulse, which starts the whole process over again. Lack of choline means that acetylcholine cannot be produced, so nerve function deteriorates with serious consequences. The therapeutic value of choline in this respect is seen in the treatment of senile dementia. Lecithin, which contains choline, has also been used.

A very recent development in the treatment of senile dementia is the use of choline as a simple dietary supplement in the form of lecithin. Experimental studies by Drs. M. J. Hirsch and R. J. Wurtman from the Massachusetts Institute of Technology showed that consumption of a single meal containing lecithin increased the levels of choline and its product acetylcholine in the brain of rats. Since acetylcholine is essential as a chemical transmitter in brain functioning, it seemed logical to try choline as a supplement in those conditions in man where acetylcholine may be deficient.

In a number of pilot studies this has been carried out on patients suffering from mental deterioration, with promising results. A typical trial was reported from Canada (*The Lancet*) when a dose of 25g of lecithin per day (i.e. 900mg choline) produced dramatic improvement in these patients. The treatment is a simple dietary one and is without side effects at the dose of 25g lecithin per day. What did emerge was that lecithin is preferable to choline as a food supplement. Choline is better absorbed as lecithin and there are more chances of side effects when choline itself is taken in high doses.

INOSITOL

This too is a constituent of lecithin, which may be regarded as its main dietary source. However, like choline, inositol and lecithin can be made by the body itself, although there do appear to be some conditions where body synthesis is insufficient. Dietary intakes and supplementation then assume importance. Supplementary doses may be as high as 1,000mg daily.

The brain and spinal cord nerves contain very high concentrations of inositol. Part of this is found in the myelin sheath, as with choline, but inositol appears to have some function not associated with its structural property. Thus Dr. C. C. Pfeiffer at the Brain Bio Centre, Princeton, New Jersey, USA, has studied the effect of inositol on brain wave patterns in schizophrenics and normal people. He claims that inositol has a similar anti-anxiety effect to that of the mild tranquilising drugs librium or meprobamate (e.g. Equagesic, Miltown). The calming effects of inositol can thus make it a possible alternative to the widely-prescribed librium and meprobamate. In this respect it is attractive to speculate that perhaps anxiety, irritability and hyperactivity may be related to a lack of inositol in the brain or some simple block in its metabolism.

All cells in the body appear to need inositol to stay healthy, but it is especially necessary for the bone marrow, eye membranes and the cells lining the gastro-intestinal tract. Unsubstantiated reports claim that it is food for stimulating good hair growth and the overcoming of baldness. These properties may be related to the role of inositol in maintaining cell structure in a healthy state.

High Blood Pressure and related conditions

Adequate intakes of all vitamins throughout life may prevent the onset of high blood pressure but, when taken at high dosage in supplementary form, some (vitamins C, E and the B vitamin choline in the form of lecithin) may also be used to treat the condition. Such natural approaches will in no way interfere with any medicinal drugs you may be taking for reducing high blood pressure and associated conditions – indeed they are almost certain to complement such drugs but they will not necessarily replace them. Always inform your practitioner if you are taking dietary or supplementary measures in addition to your medicinal drug therapy as it is possible that the latter may be reduced once the natural approach starts to benefit you.

FAT AND CHOLESTEROL CONTROL

If fat and the associated cholesterol can be controlled and metabolised normally within the body, there are lessened chances of developing high blood pressure since this can be caused by the abnormal deposition of fats on the walls of blood vessels. As these vessels become constricted, the heart pumps harder and the pressure increases, to force blood through the narrowed orifice. Several vitamins function together to prevent the abnormal deposition of fats and these should in theory both prevent the condition of high blood pressure arising and hopefully to treat the preexisting condition.

LECITHIN

This is a complex fat composed of choline, inositol and polyunsaturated fatty acids (when obtained from soya), all of which contribute to its fat-fighting qualities.

Choline is defined as a lipotropic factor, which means that it prevents fats from accumulating in the liver by facilitating the transport of these fats to the organs that require them. Liver normally contains only between 5 and 7 per cent of its weight as fat, but in the absence of choline this proportion can increase to as much as 50 per cent. Such fatty deposits, when allowed to build up in the vital organ, adversely affect its normal functioning and the ill-effects are soon felt. There are a number of diseases that can give rise to fatty liver and these include diabetes, alcoholism and protein-deficiency. Lack of choline has been implicated in the development of fatty liver by Dr. S. Mookerjea of the University of Toronto, who observed an increase of liver fats during periods of choline deprivation.

When fats are transported from the liver, they do so in the form of complex substances called phospholipids. These are composed of fats, phosphorus, sugar and choline in combination. According to experimental evidence from animal work published in the *American Journal of Clinical Nutrition*, lack of choline prevented this mechanism from operating with the result that the liver cells soon filled up with unwanted fat. Supplementation with choline not only prevented such changes but actually reserved the process and cleared the liver of accumulated fat. Human studies on infants suffering from fatty liver (*Journal of the American Medical Association*) have confirmed a similar role for choline in human beings.

It is possible that prolonged low levels of choline in the body can give rise to high blood pressure (hypertension). The compound was given to a group of patients suffering from hypertension with beneficial results according to a report in the *Journal of Vitaminology*. Typical symptoms of palpitations, dizziness and headaches disappeared within two weeks of treatment, together with reduction of the blood pressure to normal. The mechanism of this action is not known, but it could be via the nerves be controlling the blood vessels, which in turn determine the blood pressure. Other evidence suggests that low levels of choline throughout life may put some individuals on the road to hypertension in later years.

INOSITOL

We have seen above how important choline is as a lipotropic agent in ensuring that fat is kept in solution and is not deposited in the wrong places in the body. The second factor that also has this property is inositol, but it is structurally very different from choline and hence exerts its lipotropic action in a different way. The fat-fighting properties of inositol appear to act in addition to those associated with choline, so it is not surprising that both are essential in controlling fat metabolism. There are reports from the *American Heart Journal* by Drs. I. Leinwand and D. H. Moore that giving 3g of inositol daily to atherosclerotic patients resulted in a reduction of blood fats and cholesterol. Similar treatment reduced the excessive depositions of fat in those suffering from fatty liver. Despite these early reports, however, it is now accepted that the best way to restore fat metabolism to normal is by treating with both choline and inositol. Drs. D. A. Sherber and M. M. Levites reported in the *Journal of The American Medical Association* that this approach was successful in reducing cholesterol levels in all their patients subjected to the treatment.

Adequate intakes of both choline and inositol, along with polyunsaturated fatty acids, can be obtained by taking 15 to 30 grams of lecithin daily in the form of granules. Along with other measures, this can usefully be employed to treating high blood pressure and heart conditions.

Circulatory Problems

VITAMIN E

The main groups of diseases that have responded to vitamin E are essentially those of the blood circulating system, where for one reason or another, the flow of blood to an organ or muscle has been curtailed. This may be due to a blood clot (thrombosis); a narrowing of the blood vessel due to deposition of fat (atherosclerosis); a hardening of the artery (arteriosclerosis); a swollen and knotted condition of the veins (varicose veins); blood clots in the veins (thrombophlebitis).

Other conditions include high blood-pressure, heart failure, sterility, menstrual problems and ageing. In addition, some skin diseases – including severe ulceration – have been reported to respond to vitamin E treatment.

INTERMITTENT CLAUDICATION

This is the term that describes the cramping pain in the calf muscles that is produced on exercise. It is caused by a narrowing of the arteries supplying blood to the leg muscles. The restricted blood supply gives rise to the pain as the muscles become starved of oxygen. A leading article in *The Lancet* states that this is the only generally accepted use of vitamin E in medical practice. Dr. P. D. Livingstone and Dr. C. Jones reported the results of a double-blind clinical trial of vitamin E in intermittent claudication carried out at Sheffield.

Out of 17 patients who were treated with 600 i.u. of d-alpha tocopherol per day for a total period of 40 weeks, 13 showed significant improvement in their ability to walk without pain. Only 2 of the 17 patients treated with the placebo reported some improvement over a similar period. It was essential to continue treatment for at least 3 months before any improvement became apparent. It was also noted that the vitamin E-treated patients had an increased life survival rate. Eventually this research group was able to report some years later that some 1,500 patients suffering from intermittent claudication had responded favourably and significantly to tocopherol treatment.

ANGINA PECTORIS

Angina pectoris is a condition characterized by a several, constricting pain in the chest, usually radiating to one or both arms and shoulders. The pain is due to a temporary insufficiency of blood to the heart that deprives the heart muscle of oxygen. It is a similar situation to the one in intermittent claudication, except that the heart muscle itself is affected instead of the legs. In both cases the attack is relieved by rest.

According to the Shute Institute, where many thousands of angina patients have been treated with vitamin E, the angina condition usually responds in four to six weeks from the start of the treatment. The initial dose is usually 800 i.e. d–alpha tocopherol per day. If there is no improvement after six weeks on this dose, the daily intake is increased by 200 to 400 i.e. for the next six weeks.

When the dose at which the symptoms are relieved is reached, this is continued permanently. Such doses apply only when the blood pressure is controlled by drugs. Even if there is not complete relief with this treatment, it is important for anyone suffering from angina to take d–alpha tocopherol to prevent blood clots or thrombosis from forming.

CORONARY HEART DISEASE

D-alpha tocopherol helps in coronary heart disease by:
1. Dissolving the blood clot that is causing the obstruction.
2. Decreasing the oxygen needs of the whole zone of injury, so preserving its structure and function.
3. Dilating the blood vessels, so allowing more blood and hence more oxygen to reach the damaged portion of the heart. Continuous use of tocopherol following a heart attack prevents further occurrence of a blockage. Although the heart muscle that has died (known as an infarct) can never be restored, vitamin E treatment ensures that the surrounding area receives adequate oxygen and helps restore it to health.

Even when vitamin E therapy is started immediately after the heart attack, it may take a week or 10 days before any benefit is felt. A study was carried out on 22 patients by Dr. W. M. Toone and reported in the *New Zealand Journal of Medicine*. Eleven of his patients received 1,600 i.u. of d-alpha tocopherol succinate per day after their heart attacks, while the remaining eleven received a placebo. Seven of the treated patients were able to eliminate conventional medical treatment, and all felt the benefit of vitamin E. Only three of the control group were able to reduce this medical treatment.

Other studies at the Shute Institute on many hundreds of patients have indicated an overall success rate of 60 per cent of patients receiving vitamin E after a heart attack. The usual procedure is to start such patients on 800 i.u. of vitamin E per day and increase this by 200 i.u. increments every six weeks until a response is obtained. Once the dosage is established, the individual keeps it at that level for the rest of his life.

ARTERIOSLCEROSIS AND CEREBRAL THROMBOSIS

A similar dosage regime is carried out on those whose heart blood vessels are constricted by hardening, a condition usually associated with ageing. When a similar condition affects the brain blood vessels, the usual symptoms are forgetfulness, lack of concentration and impaired mental ability in the aged. In both cases vitamin E may be helpful but the addition of vitamin C at a dose of 2g to 5g per day is now known to be particularly beneficial.

A constriction of the blood supply to the brain (called cerebral thrombosis) may give rise to a stroke resulting in temporary or permanent paralysis of part of the body. Treatment with vitamin E is essentially the same as that when the heart is similarly affected. Not only does vitamin E help dissolve the obstruction but it prevents further development of a thrombosis.

VARICOSE VEINS

Another disease of the blood circulatory system is varicose veins. The conventional medical treatment for this condition is surgery. This may be avoided in some cases by treating with vitamin E but the dosage varies over a wide range. Dr. W. Shute in his book Vitamin E for Ailing and Healthy Hearts quotes many successful treatments of varicose veins with vitamin E.

The dose usually begins at 150 i.u. or 300 i.u. per day which is increased in increments of 100 i.u. every six weeks if no improvement is noted. Most people respond to 300 or 600 i.u. but some need the high dose of 800 i.u. per day before relief is obtained. One of the complications of varicose veins can be the development of ulcers (called indolent ulcers), that are very resistant to healing. Oral vitamin E has been claimed to cut down the incidence of these.

MENSTRUAL AND MENOPAUSAL PROBLEMS

There are many reports of the beneficial effects of vitamin E in relieving the painful periods suffered by some women and in normalizing the cycle where this is irregular. Heavy and scanty menstrual flows are not influenced by the vitamin.

According to the Shute Institute, vitamin E exerts its action in women by normalizing the blood levels of the female sex hormones, known as oestrogens. It dilates the blood vessels, so ensuring a good supply of blood to the womb. At the same time, the vitamin improves the heat-regulating capacity of the body, which is why it helps in excessive sweating that is often a feature of the menopause.

Menstrual abnormalities are often treated with oestrogen. However, many obstetricians and gynaecologists who have used vitamin E believe it is safer to let the vitamin stimulate the body's own production of oestrogens. There is a certain risk in treating women with sex hormones, particularly during the menopause, when their production starts to slow down. By treatment with vitamin E, it is believed that the transition to decreased production of oestrogens, with its accompanying effects, is smoother and easier. Similarly, irregular oestrogen synthesis which can give rise to problems in younger women may be normalized by vitamin E treatment.

The use of vitamin E in the menopause has been actively studied by Dr. Henry A. Gozan of New York. In the *New York State Journal of Medicine* he reported that treatment with vitamin E helped relieve the flushing, headaches and nervous symptoms associated with the menopause. There was success in easing and eliminating these distressing symptoms in 59 out of 66 patients so treated. The dosage used was 100 i.u. of the vitamin taken three times daily over a three month period.

SUNBURNT AND SCALDED SKIN

Many medical papers testify to the effectiveness of vitamin E in the form of cream or ointment in treating damaged skin, whether caused by burns, sunburn or scalding liquids. No matter what the agent is, treatment consists of covering the affected area as quickly as possible with a cream or ointment containing from 30 to 100 i.u. of vitamin E per gram. Typical treatments have been described by Dr. Wilfred E. Shute in his book *Vitamin E for Ailing and Healthy Hearts*. The time to respond varies from hours in the case of simple sunburn, to weeks when the skin is badly scalded but the important result is a minimum or complete lack of scarring.

A boy of six was scalded badly with multiple burns over his neck, torso, back, chest and thigh. An attempt at skin-grafting was not only unsuccessful but left whole areas of raw flesh that were badly infected. This persisted for 10 weeks. Treatment with vitamin E was then initiated.

After 10 days, the infection was cleared but the damaged areas remained very raw and painful. Application of vitamin E ointment was continued, along with a daily oral dose to 300 i.u. Complete healing occurred after 13 weeks. What was particularly gratifying was to find that the scars were smooth, painless and contracted into weals. Skin-grafting was not even needed.

Older people respond just as dramatically. A woman aged 58 received scalds over a wide area of her torso and the damage was worsened by leaving on her clothing, which retained the hot water next to the skin. Conventional medical treatment with brine baths failed, leaving her with a grossly infected skin. Treatment was switched to oral and topical vitamin E. Within five days healing commenced and continuation of the treatment for three months resulted in complete cure.

Dr. Wilfred E. Shute attributes the healing properties of vitamin E on the skin to three unique characteristics:
1. It lessens or removes the associated pain a few minutes after application.
2. It stops the burn from deepening, limiting the damage to the cells actually destroyed by the burning agent.
3. It stimulates rapid regeneration of new skin, giving a scar that is not painful, is of the same height as surrounding skin and is not contracted.

The mild antiseptic quality of vitamin E may help against infection but other measures are usually needed to keep the affected area clean. Once this is controlled, the healing action of the vitamin is both quick and effective.

Other conditions that may respond to Vitamin Therapy

KIDNEY STONES

The most common kind of kidney stones are formed from an insoluble mineral called calcium oxalate. This is composed of calcium and oxalic acid, both normal constituents of food. In addition, oxalic acid is produced by the body during its normal metabolic processes. Yet some people form stones and others do not, despite having similar diets. The ability to form stones depends upon two factors; first how well the calcium oxalate can be kept in solution; and second, the control of oxalic acid production. The first factor depends upon the presence of adequate magnesium since the ratio of calcium to magnesium determines the solubility of calcium oxalate. The second factor is related to vitamin B6, since when this is deficient there is an increase in oxalic acid production. Adequate pyridoxine protects by reducing the formation of this potential precipitating agent.

These observations were put to the test in a clinical study carried out at Harvard University by Drs. E. L. Prienard and S. N. Gershoff and reported in the *American Journal of Clinical Nutrition*. A total of 265 patients with histories of chronic kidney stone formation were treated with 240mg magnesium and 20mg of vitamin B6 per day. A staggering 89 per cent of these patients benefited from the course of supplementation. They stopped producing kidney stones and remained free of them while on the mineral/vitamin treatment. This simple treatment is safe and effective, but it is preferably taken in conjunction with a calcium-controlled diet, a regime that kidney stone sufferers are already familiar with.

BRONCHIAL ASTHMA

Vitamin B6 has been referred to as the anti-allergy vitamin, mainly on account of its successful use in some allergic skin diseases, in hay fever and in bronchial asthma. Comprehensive studies by a team of doctors at Nassau County Medical Centre, USA, headed by Dr. P. J. Collipp have indicated that pyridoxine is remarkably safe and effective treatment for some asthma sulferers. The clue to the treatment was provided by the observation that many asthma victims show abnormal metabolism of vitamin B6 when tested with the tryptophan loading test. Consequently, in one trial, 38 asthmatic children received 100mg of vitamin B6, twice per day and a similar number received a harmless placebo. Neither patients nor doctors knew what they were given in fact this was a true double-blind study. The effect of the treatment was assessed by noting such criteria as wheezing, difficult breathing, cough, tightness in the chest and outright asthmatic attacks.

Only starting with the second month did those receiving vitamin B6 show any definite clinical improvement over those receiving placebo. From then on, however, the improvement was maintained in every aspect of the disease. No side-effects were observed during the five-month duration of the trial. It must be stressed that existing drug treatment of the individuals continued, but as this was palliative rather than curative, (e.g. the use of bronchodilators), it was gradually phased out under medical guidance. The researchers could not explain why the vitamin has this beneficial effect, but they admit that pyridoxine appears to be acting as a drug rather than as a vitamin. It is possible that the children are suffering from a B6-dependency, so that for some reason their requirements for the vitamin are particularly high and cannot be obtained simply from the diet. Adult sufferers from asthma also benefit from a similar dosage but the positive response to the vitamin is not outstanding as that in children. These beneficial doses of vitamin B6 should only be taken under supervision of a qualified practitioner.

INSECT BITES

Those who suffer from the excessive attentions of insects can be helped by vitamin BI according to a report in Medical Letters and subsequent reports. Out of 100 sufferers in one trial, more than 70 per cent reported that on an intake of 75 to 100mg daily, insects bothered them little or not at all. It is highly unlikely that at this level of intake the thiamine is acting in its true vitamin role, but rather as a therapeutic internal insect repellent. No side-effects were noted in this trial. This protective effect has not been noted in everyone probably because some people may require even higher intakes of the vitamin. It does appear likely though that the vitamin functions by finding its way to the skin where its odour, detectable bv insects but not by human beings, may act as a deterrent.

CARPAL TUNNEL SYNDROME

Carpal tunnel syndrome is due to a compression of the median nerve as it enters the palm of the hand. This causes pain and numbness in the index and middle fingers and weakness of the muscle of the thumb. The condition is relatively common and can affect either one or both hands. Women are most affected and the syndrome is often seen during the last third period of pregnancy. Vitamin B6 has been found to relieve the condition. The usual dose is 50mg of the vitamin daily during the first three months of pregnancy and this is usually sufficient to prevent the syndrome in the last three months. Vitamin B6 at this level must not be taken by a pregnant woman without the knowledge of her doctor. In other people, 50-250mg of vitamin B6 daily may be needed to relieve the pain of the syndrome and the dose must be continued for at least 12 weeks. Stiffness in the fingers of diabetics will often be relieved by vitamin B6 at daily doses between 50 and 100mg. The problem in diabetic children may be overcome by daily doses of 25mg of the vitamin.

Food allergies and Supplementation

Foods may provoke a wide variety of allergic symptoms by multiple mechanisms but the release of histamine is one of the most important. Histamine is found in nearly all of the tissues of the body but is associated mainly with mast cells. During inflammation and allergic response, mast cells release a variety of chemicals amongst which is histamine which has pronounced pharmacological activity that serves to protect the body. However, when the histamine is released under abnormal stimulus such as allergens in food, the responsive mechanisms can cause undesirable symptoms. Hence the development of anti-histamines that neutralise the effect of the released substance.

It has been established that when blood vitamin C levels are low, blood histamine levels are high. Giving supplemental vitamin C causes reduction of these high histamine concentrations. This was observed in

1981 when 437 normal subjects deliberately reduced their blood levels of vitamin C by withdrawing it from their diets. As the levels of vitamin decreased so whole blood histamine levels increased. Once ascorbate concentration dropped below 0.7mg per 100ml blood, the increase in blood histamine levels was highly significant. In another study, when vitamin C blood levels were low or histamine blood levels were high, a daily dose of one gram of the vitamin restored histamine levels to normal in only 3 days. The same amount of the vitamin given along with 10mg vitamin BI reduced the symptoms of allergic rhinitis substantially in 75% of the people affected.

The fat soluble vitamin E also is regarded as an antihistamine vitamin. Volunteers who had severe swelling at the site after injection of histamine had a much reduced response when pretreated with 400 i.u. vitamin E for 5-7 days. Vitamin B12 is a water-soluble vitamin that has exhibited anti-histamine activity in conditions of intractable asthma, chronic urticaria and allergic dermatitis - all conditions that can be induced by food ingredients. However, the vitamin must be in a high potency injection into the muscle (1000μg) since because of limited absorption, oral tablets will not give high enough body levels.

Monosodium glutamate (MSG) widely used in food preparation as a flavour enhancer is also one of the most common allergens in the diet. Taking vitamin C before food containing MSG will protect adverse allergic effects of the flavour enhancer which can be very distressing to some people causing serious flushing, headaches, dizziness and nerve problems. MSG sensitivity can also be controlled by vitamin B6. In an experimental double-blind study reported in 1981, a daily dose of 50mg vitamin B6 was given to 9 students who had exhibited strong allergic response to MSG previously while 3 researchers received placebo. After 12 weeks therapy with the vitamin those who suffered from MSG no longer did so and those on placebo continued to respond to it.

Bioflavonoids, notably catechin and quercetin, are found in all diets but are particularly rich in fruits and vegetables. Like vitamin C, which they invariably accompany in the food, bioflavonoids are excellent oral anti-histamines. Catechin for example functions in two ways. First, it inhibits the release of histamine from the mast cells and second, it inhibits the enzyme needed to convert the amino acid histidine into histamine. This conversion is a continuous process in the mast cells. Catechin has been given to people with food allergies and as long as it was given before the allergenic food, it prevented an allergic response. Quercetin, another bioflavonoid in our food, acts in a similar manner and its effect in the pure state is so great that it has been used to suppress the symptoms of allergic asthma. Although our diet provides both allergenic substances and antiallergen constituents, the balance is usually in favour of the former which is why some people will continue to respond adversely to these undesirable substances. Fortunately, other food constituents like the vitamins and bioflavonoids when taken in amounts far beyond those found in the diet can help neutralise the effects of allergenic food substances.

How safe are Vitamins?

As far as self-help with supplementary vitamins is concerned only two of them, A and D, should be regarded as likely to give rise to toxic side-effects when taken in very high doses. For this reason the UK authorities have suggested, and indeed in some cases have legislated for, a maximum supplementary daily intake of vitamin A of 7,500 i.u. (2.25mg). In the case of vitamin D, no more than 400 i.u. (10μg), should be taken on a daily basis. On prescription of course, and hence under medical supervision, higher potencies can be obtained and taken.

The limits above apply only to products containing vitamins A and D that are available on general sale and the golden rule is – take these supplements only at the daily dose recommended on the pack. There is no point in anyone in this country and in the Western world in general taking more than 7,500 i.u. vitamin A and 400 i.u. vitamin D on a regular basis. Remember that these vitamins are being taken in addition to those in the diet and the supplementary limits take dietary intakes into account. Dosing yourself with more than the recommended amount will do no more good than taking that suggested on the pack. If you feel you need much higher intakes of vitamin A and D for one reason or another then you obviously need professional medical advice.

To these two fat-soluble vitamins must now be added a water-soluble one, pyridoxine or vitamin B6. Some side-effects have been reported in people taking massive doses of pyridoxine on a daily basis over many months. Most of these individuals were taking between 2,000 and 6,000mg of the vitamin daily. One case of side-effects in a person taking 500mg daily for a long period has also been reported but this response should be regarded as most unusual.

When we look at these reports in perspective they can be seen as representing quite abnormal and unnecessary potencies of the vitamin. Daily intakes below these have not been reported as causing any ill-effects in the many trials where pyridoxine has been taken to treat premenstrual syndrome or the side-effects of the contraceptive pill. It would need for example, 20 of the highest potency vitamin B6 preparations (100mg) available in the UK, taken daily for many months, to allow the lower toxicity level of 2,000mg to be reached. Much higher potencies are available in the USA which probably explains why this is where toxicity problems were reported.

Self-help with all vitamins can be beneficial to many people but remember to take only the dosage recommended on the pack unless higher intakes are suggested by a medical or other practitioner.

5 | Getting the most from your Vitamins

Despite the ever-growing number of people who feel the need to take extra vitamins in tablet or soft-gelatine capsule form, there is no doubt that our basic needs for these micronutrients should be from the daily diet. Adequate daily requirements of vitamins can be met solely from the food, on the assumption that this is freshly picked, cooked expertly with an eye to preserving the vitamins, and eaten as soon as possible after preparations. Such considerations are fine in theory but often impossible to achieve in practice, yet a few simple rules will ensure that you are getting the most from the vitamins in your diet.

The vitamin B complex and vitamin C are all water-soluble so that when boiling food, more losses are due to leaching into the water than simple destruction. As long as the water is then used in the preparation of a sauce or gravy the leached vitamins are retrieved and contribute an important proportion of the day's requirements. Short term boiling in a minimum amount of water retains far more vitamins in all vegetables than long term boiling in a lot of water. However, the steaming and pressure cooking of green vegetables is to be preferred to boiling, although the difference in vitamins leached from root vegetables is not as great when cooking losses for these three methods are compared.

Deep freezing of foods represents a good way of preserving vitamins but the process is preceded by blanching which itself can cause some preliminary loss. Microwave blanching causes less damage to vitamin levels than hot water treatment because of the leaching losses referred to above. Don't forget though that the act of thawing allows vitamins to escape into the thawed water. This is of less importance in frozen vegetables which can be cooked immediately from the frozen state but losses can be significant in meats and poultry where thawing periods of up to 24 hours are usually recommended before cooking commences. Utilizing the thawed liquors will help you recapture those vitamins that got away. Losses by leaching of boiled frozen vegetables are just as large as those when fresh vegetables are boiled, sometimes they are greater since the acts of freezing and thawing ruptures cells, allowing more of the contents to escape.

Studies on the preservatives of vitamins during microwave cooking have given variable results. For example vitamin C is better retained in broccoli, achieved by taking an effective prolonged (or sustained) release formulation. A good product will release its vitamin steadily at an even rate over the necessary 6, 8 and 12-hour period in exactly the way they would be if present in food. These, too, are best taken with food because then the ingredients of the tablet or capsule will move along the digestive tract at the same rate as the food it accompanies.

One of the more controversial subjects in vitamin supplementation is whether naturally-derived vitamins offer advantages over the synthetic variety. If we look at the evidence available there is little doubt that the scales come down in favour of the natural vitamins. We get more out of these for the following reasons. Most vitamins can exist in two forms, which for convenience we can refer to as right-handed (d) and left-handed (l). This is simply a quirk of their chemical structure and the difference may appear to be minimal when viewed in a chemical light. Nevertheless, in terms of biological activity, the body is very selective and it can use only one of the forms, the other being virtually useless. Not surprisingly, in foods and other natural sources, nature provides the correct biological form of the vitamin. Sometimes it is the d-form, other times the l-form, there are no hard and fast rules, but the natural form represents that most efficiently used by the body. A prime example is d-alpha tocopherol, the natural form of vitamin E, which on a milligram for milligram basis is 49 per cent more active than the synthetic dl variety. Nature is rather more clever than the chemist when it comes to making vitamin E. Whereas in nature the d-form alone is produced, the chemist can only make the dl-form, i.e. 50 per cent of each type. It is possible for the chemist to resolve his dl-vitamin E and isolate just the d-form but his yield is only 50 per cent and the l-form is wasted. It is just not worth the expense to separate the two types so the chemist offers the mixture and allows the body to select the form of vitamin E it can use.

Although d-alpha tocopherol is regarded as the natural form of vitamin E, it does not occur in nature on its own. Food sources of the vitamin invariably contain a mixture of four different types called d-alpha, d-beta, d-gamma and d-delta-tocopherols. In most biological test systems the most active vitamin E on a milligram for milligram basis is d-alpha tocopherol. However, in terms of anti-oxidant activity, which represents possibly the most important protective function of vitamin E, d-delta tocopherol is the most potent. Such differences reflect the wisdom of ensuring an intake, dietary or supplementary, of all the tocopherols since it could be wrong to assess the activity of the whole group simply on one criterion or another.

Vitamin C (ascorbic acid) appears rather easier to deal with because this is one case where the chemist can synthesize in the laboratory exactly the type of the vitamin that occurs in nature, namely l-ascorbic acid. Hence it is well-nigh impossible for anyone to detect the difference between vitamin C isolated from the acerola cherry and that produced in a laboratory because they are both the l-form. Nevertheless, there are differences in the way the body can use the vitamin C present in acerola powder and that present as pure ascorbic acid. The secret lies in the substances that accompany the vitamin in the natural source that are not present in the synthetic variety.

These substances are the bioflavonoids which are always associated with vitamin C when it occurs naturally. The body, too, appears to require them for the most efficient utilization of vitamin C in some of its functions. As the bioflavonoids (sometimes called vitamin P) and ascorbic acid function together in the maintenance of the health and integrity of the blood vessels it is sensible to take both together in tablets or capsules as they are taken thus in the diet.

The example of vitamin C and the bioflavonoids illustrates neatly the prime difference between naturally occurring and synthetic vitamins. The former are superior in their biological action because they are presented in their natural environment. This means that even in tablet or capsule form, vitamin C is best utilized when it is accompanied by rose hip powder, acerola cherry powder or some other natural source of the vitamin and the bioflavonoids. The B vitamins are more efficiently assimilated in the presence of yeast or liver powder. Vitamin E is preferred in the oil from which it is derived, be it wheat germ or soya.

Not only are such preparations presenting the vitamins in the environment that nature supplies them in but there is always the possibility that the accompanying substances confer greater activity on the vitamin (as with vitamin C and the bioflavonoids). Yeast is a complex organism containing all the B vitamins, apart from vitamin B 12, but it is possible that there are also present some, as yet, unknown factors that need to accompany the vitamins we already know about. There could even be more unidentified vitamins present that you can obtain only from natural sources.

There is, however, one vitamin that is probably utilized better from tablets than from the food itself. This is folic acid, which in the natural form exists both as the free acid and as the acid conjugated or combined with glutamic acid residues of up to six in number. Free folic acid is far better absorbed than conjugated folic acid. Hence if a food supplies mainly the conjugated variety not much of it will actually be assimilated by the body. Peanuts for example contain in 100g only 28μg of free folic acid, but 82μg of the conjugated form which is less readily absorbed. On the other hand, 100 gram of cabbage yields 60μg of the free form along with only 30μg of the conjugated acid, which means that most of the vitamin is readily absorbed. In tablet form, folic acid is usually presented as the free acid so we would expect a higher efficiency of absorption.

It has often been said the vitamin of the B complex are better utilized when all are presented in the same formulation in the correct balance as that found in foods. This is true up to a point as for example in the situation, not uncommon, where there is a mild deficiency of the B vitamins across the whole spectrum. A poor diet or a stress situation is more likely to cause a mild deficiency of the whole complex so it is not unreasonable to supplement with all of them. Situations do arise, however, where a particular deficiency is induced usually by treatment with a specific medicinal drug. The contraceptive pill, for example, is notorious in increasing the requirements of vitamin B6 in the female. Taking it and this vitamin alone, in potencies of 50mg upwards, is often sufficient to overcome the mild depression associated with this form of contraception. In such cases because the synthetic hormones are inducing a specific deficiency, we need only replace that particular vitamin, and there is no upset in the balance of the other B vitamins.

Similarly, folic acid blood levels are sometimes reduced by the action of the drug sulphasalazine, used to treat ulcerative colitis. Taking aspirin for prolonged periods at high dose will reduce specifically the body vitamin C levels. Hence it would appear to be a sensible measure to supplement each of these drug treatments with the particular vitamin that is missing but this will not upset the balance of any of the other vitamins.

These are just a few examples where medicinal drugs affect the status of a specific vitamin in the body, but as we have seen there are many others. Once the vitamin deficiency is known it can be treated by simple supplementation to restore the body levels of that affected vitamin.

The best way to make the most of your fat-soluble vitamins is to remember that they are fats and that any factor upsetting fat absorption will have a deleterious effect upon the body status of the vitamins. Since they are fat-soluble, vitamins A, D, E and K will be retained in the body longer than water-soluble vitamins and will be stored in the liver and fatty tissues. It is because they are stored that, of all vitamins, A and D are regarded as the most toxic in high potency. Body levels can build up over a period of time until eventually a dangerous concentration is reached. By the same token, once this level is reached, even when they are no longer eaten, it takes a long time for the tissues to rid themselves of the excess vitamins. The safest way to get the most from vitamins A and D is not to go beyond the maximum daily intake recommended by the manufacturers. This is particularly so in the supplementation of babies and infants.

Any condition, drug or treatment such as liquid paraffin which can reduce the absorption of fats or can immobilise them will lead to deficiencies of the fat-soluble vitamins. If the interfering factor is long-lasting it could become essential to take these vitamins in some other way. One is by injection but a more feasible procedure for self-treatment is to take them as water-solubilized preparations. In this way the fat-absorption pathway is bypassed and the vitamins are treated as though they were water-soluble.

One of the biggest problems for those who wish to treat themselves with vitamins is how to get high levels of B12 into the body. This vitamin is unique because it requires attachment to a specific protein called intrinsic factor, which is produced in the parietal cells of the stomach, before it can be absorbed. The combination takes place in the stomach from whence the complex moves down to the part of the small intestine known as the ileum where in a specific area the whole complex is absorbed. The amount of vitamin B12 absorbed by this mechanism is unlikely to be above 8µg from a single dose since intrinsic factor production is limited and the receptor sites in the ileum soon become saturated.

However, in addition to this unique mechanism, some B12 is absorbed by simple diffusion. Radioactive tracer techniques carried out on pernicious anaemia patients, who have lost the ability to make intrinsic factor indicate that not more than 1 per cent of a single dose of the vitamin is absorbed up to the 1,000µg level. Above this the percentage absorbed drops even further. What this means is that a normal individual taking 100µg of B12 in a single tablet will absorb only 9 (i.e. 1+8) µg. The rest is wasted. A person suffering from pernicious anaemia is unlikely to absorb more than one µg. There is a popular fallacy that sorbitol enhances the absorption of B12, even in pernicious anaemia patients, but the evidence for this is far from satisfactory.

We must, therefore, conclude that the only way in which to get high levels of B12 into the body is by intramuscular injection. Even by this route, probably 40 per cent of a 1,000µg dose of cyanocobalamin is excreted in the first 24 hours but thereafter the excretion rate drops dramatically. The best type of vitamin B12 for intramuscular injection is hydroxocobalamin. Because this differs slightly in structure it is retained in the body to a much greater extent than cyanocobalamin. Pernicious anaemia patients who require regular injections of the vitamin usually respond satisfactorily to 1,000µg of hydroxo-cobalamin every two months, or to 1,000µg of cyanocobalamin monthly.

We have seen that once supplementation is decided upon we can, with a little thought, make the most of the many preparations that are available. The factors controlling our choice are to a large extent personal. Do we require an all-round multivitamin intake simply to insure against deficiency? Perhaps a rapid high-level intake is needed. Are we creating specific deficiencies by our way of life, whether they be due to lifestyle or medicinal drugs, and if so what are they? Let us make sure that we know exactly why we feel we need the vitamins we are taking. Once that is established, common sense will usually dictate how we may make the best use of them.

OTHER BOOKS FROM AMBERWOOD PUBLISHING ARE:

Aromatherapy – A Guide for Home Use by Christine Westwood. All you need to know about essential oils and using them. £1.99.

Aromatherapy – For Stress Management by Christine Westwood. Covering the use of essential oils for everyday stress-related problems. £2.99.

Aromatherapy – For Healthy Legs and Feet by Christine Westwood. A comprehensive guide to the use of essential oils for the treatment of legs and feet, including illustrated massage instructions. £2.99.

Aromatherapy – Simply For You by Marion Del Gaudio Mak. A clear, simple and comprehensive guide to Aromatherapy for beginners. £1.99.

Plant Medicine – A Guide for Home Use by Charlotte Mitchell MNIMH. A guide to home use giving an insight into the wonderful healing qualities of plants. £2.99.

Woman Medicine – Vitex Agnus Castus by Simon Mills MA, FNIMH. The wonderful story of a herb that has been used for centuries in the treatment of women's problems. £2.99.

Ancient Medicine – Ginkgo Biloba by Dr Desmond Corrigan BSc(Pharms), MA, Phd, FLS, FPSI. Improved memory, circulation and concentration are associated in this book with medicine from this fascinating tree. £2.99.

Indian Medicine – The Immune System by Desmond Corrigan BSc(Pharms), MA, Phd, FLS, FPSI. An intriguing account of the history and science of the plant called Echinacea and its power to influence the immune system. £2.99.

Herbal First Aid by Andrew Chevallier BA, MNIMH. A beautifully clear reference book of natural remedies and general first aid in the home. £2.99.

Natural Taste – Herbal Teas, A Guide for Home Use by Andrew Chevallier BA, MNIMH. This beautifully illustrated book containing a comprehensive compendium of Herbal Teas gives information on how to make it, its benefits, history and folklore. £2.99.

Causes & Prevention of Vitamin Deficiency by Dr Leonard Mervyn BSc, PhD, C.Chem, FRCS. A home guide to the Vitamin content of foods and the depletion caused by cooking, storage and processing. It includes advice for those whose nutritional needs are increased due to lifestyle, illness etc. £2.99.

Eyecare Eyewear – For Better Vision by Mark Rossi Bsc, MBCO. A complete guide to eyecare and eyewear including an assessment of the types of spectacles and contact lenses available and the latest corrective surgical procedures. £3.99.